MUHAMMAD ALI:
IN FIGHTER'S HEAVEN

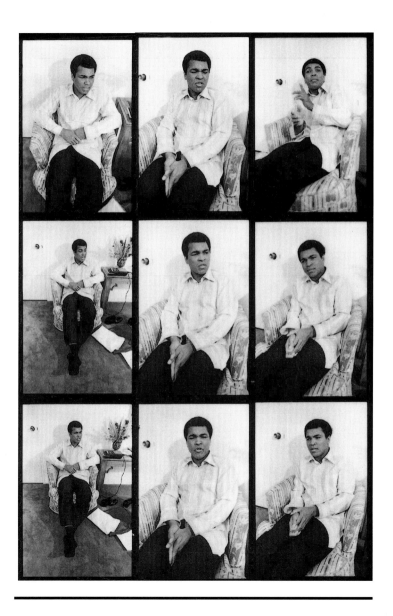

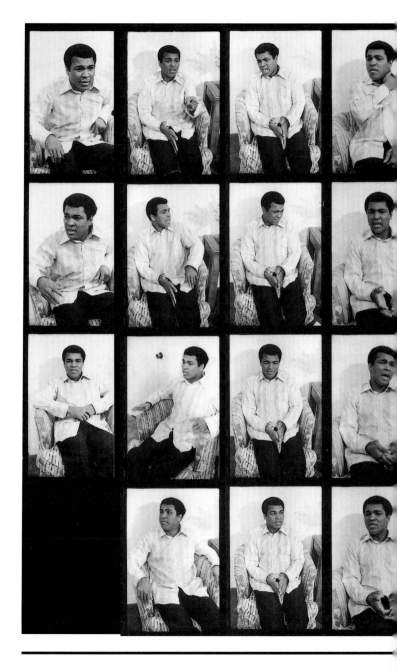

MUHAMMAD ALI: IN FIGHTER'S HEAVEN

Victor Bockris

**With video documentary by Anton Perich
and Contact strips by Raeanne Rubenstein**

 Hutchinson London

1 3 5 7 9 10 8 6 4 2

This edition first published in 1998 by Hutchinson

Random House (UK) Limited

20 Vauxhall Bridge Road, London SW1V 2SA

Random House Australia (Pty) Limited

20 Alfred Street, Milsons Point, Sydney,

New South Wales 2061, Australia

Random House South Africa (Pty) Limited

Endulini, 5A Jubilee Road, Parktown 2193, South Africa

A CIP record for this book is available from the British Library

Papers used by Random House UK Limited are natural, recyclable
products made from wood grown in sustainable forests.

The manufacturing processes conform to the environmental regulations
of the country of origin.

ISBN 0 09 180 1958

Designed by Anthony Cohen

Typeset in Bembo and Hoeffler Champion

Printed and bound in Great Britain

by Butler & Tanner, Frome, Somerset

TO ELVIS PRESLEY

CONTENTS

INTRODUCTION
THE FIRST ENCOUNTER

When I first met Muhammad Ali in the summer of 1973 he was thirty-one years old and a bundle of contradictions. While making a point of devoting his life to Black Muslim principles, he inhabited a wealthy home in a white Philadelphia suburb, and money flowed through his hands like water. He was married to his second wife Veronica, a tall, graceful black woman who adhered to his religious principles and had borne him two daughters and a son. Yet his sexual activities beyond the family fold were legend. He bought cars like Elvis; one day I would see him reclining in the back of a white stretch Lincoln limousine, the next he would be stooping into the back of a brand new green Rolls Royce to retrieve a sheaf of papers. He also owned several aeroplanes and maintained a luxurious, privately commissioned touring bus in which he and his entourage often drove to his fights.

In these details, apart from the affiliation with the Black Muslims, his life appeared little different from previous heavyweight champions. However, there was, and is, a lot more to Ali than meets the eye. Although few people knew it then, Ali's plan, after regaining the heavyweight championship in Zaire in 1974, was to retire from boxing and travel around the world delivering the kinds of lectures and poems that appear later in my book.

Prior to this, some students at Oxford had passed around a petition voting Ali the next visiting professor of poetry. This was

The author with Muhammad in 1973 at the time of the first interview.

the sort of thing the press would jump on, and he would enjoy playing along with. The previous recipient of the award had been W. H. Auden. As Ali explained, 'They said I only had to go there twice a year to give speeches. The salary couldn't pay my laundry bills, but a boxer has never been a professor of poetry at Oxford University, so I said I would do it.'

At the time I was a penniless poet living in Philadelphia, trying to make a living by interviewing celebrities I thought I could learn something from for national magazines. I wasn't a committed boxing fan, but, like everyone in the world, I knew **9**

Muhammad in 1973 at Fighter's Heaven with one of his cars

Muhammad Ali, had seen him beat Sonny Liston in 1964 and watched him battle his way back as a contender for George Foreman's heavyweight crown, after having been suspended in 1967 from boxing because of his refusal to be inducted into the army during the Vietnam conflict.

When I read the piece about Ali and Oxford in a local paper, I knew I had found my subject.

Three days after I phoned him at Fighter's Heaven, his training camp in Deerlake, Pennsylvania, a 1½ hour drive from Philadelphia, I found myself sitting in his log-cabin kitchen

He was definitely planning to quit boxing and begin the second half of his career. 'They ain't seen nothing yet!' he assured me. 'They just seen a little boxing. They ain't seen the real Muhammad Ali!'

underneath a sign saying 'Don't criticise the coffee, you may be old and weak yourself one day'.

Ali was a quick study. He realised within the first hour of our conversation that I was somebody who might actually print what he said, because I seemed, as I was, highly amused by his scintillating talk. He turned our first one and a half hour interview into an eight hour marathon. As we were leaving the kitchen after the first round of taping, Ali shouted excitedly, 'Wanna go for a ride on the bus?' 'Yes!' I yelled.

One hour later, as the bus climbed back from Highway 61 up Muhammad's Mountain to Fighter's Heaven, Ali told me I was the 'young, white, college educated long hair' he had been looking for, who could take his message to all the other 'young, white, college long hairs'. During the late sixties when he was not allowed to box, Ali had made part of his much needed income lecturing at colleges just like Timothy Leary, Allen Ginsberg, Andy Warhol and the other leading counterculture figures. 'Now,' he told me, he was getting ready to be the 'next black Billy Graham'.

As soon as Ali beat George Foreman in the 'Rumble in the Jungle', as he was already calling it, and won back the world heavyweight championship, he was definitely planning to quit

11

boxing and begin the second half of his career. 'They ain't seen nothing yet!' he assured me, popping his eyes out in a put-on bug-eyed stare. 'They just seen a little boxing!' he shouted. 'They ain't seen the real Muhammad Ali!'

I was invited to come and visit him at his camp whenever I wanted to. Over the next year I went up there at least ten times, taping on each occasion a conversation with Ali, in between getting to know the other people in his world.

The little book that grew out of those meetings and conversations with Ali was the brainchild of Gerard Malanga, who was an acquisitions editor at the legendary publisher Maurice Girodias' (*Candy, Naked Lunch, Lolita*) last publishing venture, the Freeway Press. Malanga had been the first literary figure to recognise Ali as a poet in his 1963 edition of the Wagner Literary Review. *Ali: Fighter, Poet, Prophet* was published, the very day Ali beat Foreman on 30 October, 1974. We had, of course, the traditional lunch publishers take their authors to on such occasions.

However, Girodias had left his wallet at the office, so I ended up paying for our 'victory' lunch with my last fifty dollars. Two weeks later, Freeway Press went bankrupt. Because Maurice had not paid his printer for months, the infuriated man shredded the fifty-thousand copies of my book he had not delivered to the distributor. We estimated that one to two-thousand copies saw the light of day. It was never reviewed.

Shortly thereafter I was personally able to give Ali a box of two hundred copies of the book in his New York hotel, the Essex House, on Central Park South, and walked down the big street with him as he looked through it, surrounded by a screaming, hysterical crowd.

Still, *Ali: Fighter, Poet, Prophet* held a special place in my heart for the following twenty-three years. It was my first book, my first baby, and I knew that Ali had appreciated it because when a long

'Yeah! I ride em, man. I can ride like Roy Rogers! Can I ride? You stick around a little while, you gonna see me ride!'

section had been published in Penthouse magazine, he had thanked me warmly for printing faithfully what he had said.

I met Ali again in 1977, when, as a go-between, I accompanied Andy Warhol to Fighter's Heaven. Warhol had been commissioned to paint his portrait. In the three years since Zaire, Ali had defended his heavyweight crown an unheard of nine times. One of these fights included the 1975 'Thrilla in Manila', his third encounter with Joe Frazier. Ali won, but took intense punishment, making him feel 'closer to death than I have ever been'. And it appears that it was this fight which began the slide into the damaged state Ali must endure for the rest of his life.

Ali's handlers kept him boxing far too long, and his deterioration was already obvious long before those last two horrific contests with Holmes and Berbick in the early 1980s. The Warhol visit was a pastiche of my earlier encounters. Ali read a poem and delivered a lecture before we could make our escape. The poem had little meaning and the lecture was alarming. After completing his photographic session, before our car cleared the periphery of the camp, Warhol turned to me and asked insistently, 'But is he intelligent? Is he intelligent?!'

When I knew him in 1973-74, Muhammad Ali was at the top of his game. He sparkled with energy, intelligence and a surreal sense of humour. You can see this dignified, beautiful and charismatic hero in Leon Gast's Oscar-winning documentary *When We Were Kings*, much of which was shot during the time this book was being recorded. And you can hear Ali's captivating and distinctive voice. In one scene he cracks at the camera, 'Only last week I murdered a rock, injured a stone, hospitalised a brick. I'm so mean I make medicine sick.' This prompted the New Yorker's film

> **Ali's handlers kept him boxing far too long, and his deterioration was already obvious long before those last two horrific contests with Holmes and Berbick.**

critic, Anthony Lane, to write, 'So now we know. Among his many other accomplishments, Muhammad Ali invented rap.' Writing about the film in the New York Times, Will Sower concluded, 'In 1974 Mr Ali was one of the world's most brilliant talkers, especially on the issue of black identity.'

Muhammad in 1973 at Fighter's Heaven with Victor Bockris.

After 1981, when Ali literally shuffled out of the ring, twice beaten by former sparring partners, he tailspinned into a painful freefall from fame. One day at Andy Warhol's New York Factory I met the soccer player, Pele. He told me that Ali was having a terrible time adjusting to the loss of the limelight; more seriously he was developing physical ailments which made it hard for him to speak clearly. The chances of becoming 'the next Billy Graham' disappeared as suddenly as the big paydays. The sportscasters and boxing writers who had done so well out of Ali when he was making it, knew the truth and faded away. Not only was Ali in and out of hospitals, but much of his money simply vanished. For his final fight, he received less than 10% of the purse.

As far as the sports industry was concerned, the less said about Ali in the eighties the better. Never mind that he had singlehandedly rejuvenated a dying sport, making many millions of dollars for the promoters. He was of no use to them anymore. As far as they were concerned, the sooner he died the sooner they would be safe from any allegations of financial misconduct.

Surprisingly, but perhaps fittingly, it was rock stars who began the rejuvenation of his career, which now has him travelling around the world on a mission for peace and goodwill. Maybe it **15** was because in the eighties the rock community woke up to what Ali had signalled ten years earlier. Part of Ali's genius in the seventies had been his worldwide, as opposed to national, viewpoint combined with his ability to maximize his energy from the adulation he received. When he was the most famous man in the world, Ali took his fights beyond sports onto the world stage. Speaking into Gast's camera in Zaire he said he was fighting for Africa, for poor people, 'for the little brothers sleeping on floors who got nothing to eat . . . I want to win for the wine-heads, dope addicts, prostitutes, people who got nothing, who don't know their own history. I can help these people by winning.'

Patti Smith had always celebrated Ali, saying he was the poet she would most like to give a reading with, and treating her concerts like his fights. In the mid-eighties, Madonna often mentioned Ali as an inspiration. New York's radio king Howard Stern and his sidekick Robin Quivers were also big Ali fans. In the nineties ex-vocalist of *Jane's Addiction* and *Porno for Pyros*, now creator of *Lolapalooza*, Perry Farrel, said of Ali: 'The man burned himself up. He made everything look so easy. Something that's so difficult, taking shots to the face.'

These accounts were written twenty and twenty-three years ago. Reading them now, particularly in light of the renewed interest in Ali with the success of *When We Were Kings*, and David Miller's *The Tao of Muhammad Ali*, gives a unique view of Ali the rapper-writer who could have been. In a third work, Thomas Hauser's *Muhammad Ali in Perspective*, there is a photograph taken in 1994 by Ali's friend and personal photographer, Howard Bingham. It shows Ali and his fourth and most wonderful wife, Lonnie, reading an extremely rare, mint condition copy of my original book. Ali holds it open in one hand with a serene expression on his face while Lonnie, kneeling on the floor to his left, beams up at him. The caption by the black senator Julian Bond reads: 'Ali doesn't say as much now as he did before, but he doesn't have to. He said it all, and said it when almost no one else would.'

HIGHWAY 61
REVISITED

HIGHWAY 61 REVISITED

Thirty miles outside Reading in northern
Pennsylvania, Highway 61 winds through a series of
small towns nestled among pine forests and rolling
fields. Tractors from local farms rumble along the edge
of a four-lane road lined by a series of clapboard ice
cream stands, scattered garages and battered
advertisements until, two miles past the Deer Lake
Motel, a large white sign with red letters points across the road up
a steep hill to 'ALI'S CAMP'.

Every Sunday, a number of tourists turn off Highway 61 and
follow the dirt drive up a wooded hill. Halfway up, the track turns
sharply to the left, then right; around the corner, the driver
catches sight of a large parking lot cut into the hillside on his left
and, nailed to the trunk of an oak tree on his right, another red
sign reading 'WELCOME TO ALI'S CAMP' points down a sharp
incline towards a group of log cabins.

Parking, the visitor gets out of
his car, crosses the drive and
follows the sign down toward the
cabins. He glances to his right at
a small red stable and corral in
which two workhorses are
grazing. On his left, in front of
the first log cabin, he sees a black
boulder six feet long, four feet
high, with the name JOE LOUIS
painted across it in large white
capital letters. As it leads around

**The driveway grows
narrow, bordered on the
right by a series of
similar boulders, each
bearing the name of a
great boxer: Jersey Joe
Walcott, Sugar Ray
Robinson, Rocky
Marciano, Archie Moore,
Kid Gavilan . . .**

18

to the right of the log cabin, the driveway grows narrow, bordered on the right by a series of similar boulders, each bearing the name of a great boxer: Jersey Joe Walcott, Sugar Ray Robinson, Rocky Marciano, Archie Moore, Kid Gavilan . . . Beyond the rocks, the ground falls off in steep, thickly wooded slopes. The walls of the long low cabin border the left side of the drive until, rounding the corner of the cabin, the visitor enters a large rectangular courtyard overlooking the highway and surrounding hills.

The driveway picks up again diagonally across the courtyard, climbing – between another long log cabin to the left and a smaller cabin with a chimney to the right – up past a fourth cabin set into the hill. It ends in front of a chicken coop on the border of trees which rise to the hilltop. As he stands on the edge of the courtyard, the visitor can see in front of him, in the middle of the yard, an enormous stone fireplace. To the left of the small log cabin, he notices a massive iron bell hanging from two dark poles jutting twenty feet into the clear country air.

20   The second, larger log cabin on his left has another sign beside the door, and he walks closer to examine it, reading: CORETTA'S KITCHEN. He turns back and looks around. Long wooden benches hewn from massive tree trunks are set around the courtyard beside an early American carriage and the frame of a large covered wagon.

Just then a dark green Rolls Royce appears silently around the corner of the first cabin. A dapper black man climbs out and, greeting the visitor, begins to lead him around the camp, pointing out the sights. They enter the first log cabin. The visitor looks around a small, low-ceilinged room with a day-bed propped against the wall on his right. To his left, a door leads into a large shower-room. Across the room, through another door, he can see a large, immaculate, modern gymnasium.

On the wall to his left, a life-size cardboard black and white photograph depicts a slight, sixteen-year-old, Golden Gloves champion Cassius Clay in a boxing pose.

Stepping into the gym, he notices numerous memorabilia of Muhammad Ali's life and career. On the wall to his left, a life-size cardboard black and white photograph depicts a slight, sixteen-year-old, Golden Gloves champion Cassius Clay in a boxing pose. Past the photographs is a full-length mirror, then more photographs of Ali in action, taken from the covers of *Time, Life, Newsweek, Sports Illustrated*, and many other magazines. Across the gym, another large portrait hangs beside a huge pair of golden gloves with 'Floyd Patterson' inscribed in black ink across the wrists. In the center of the gym is a full scale championship ring, with a heavy bag hanging from the ceiling in front of it and a second light bag positioned near the right wall.

After a minute the guide turns and, walking back through the small sleeping room, leads the visitor out on to the courtyard again, taking him toward the cabin marked CORETTA'S KITCHEN. Inside is a large, cafeteria-style room, with three long tables on the right, two long stoves, a double sink, two large refrigerators, cupboards, a chopping table, and two tall aluminium coffee machines on the left. On the wall opposite the door is a fourth sign, again painted in red letters, announcing:

Rules of My **KYTCHEN**

1 **PLEASE TO KEEP OUTE** except on express permission of cooke

2 **COOKE** shall designate pot scourers pan polishers peelers scrapers and COOKE has supreme **AUTHORITY AT ALL TIMES**.

3 **NO REMARKS AT ALL WILL BE TOLORATED** concerning the blackening of toast the weakness of soupe or the strength of the garlic stewe.

4 What goes in stews & soups is **NOBODY'S** dam business.

5 If you **MUST** sticke your finger in something stick it in the garbage disposal.

6 **DON'T CRITICIZE** the coffee you may be olde and weak yourself someday.

7 **ANYONE** bringinge guests in for dinner without **PRIOR NOTICE** will be awarded thwacks on skull with sharpe object.

8 **PLEASE WAITE** Rome wasn't burnt in a day and it takes awhile to burne the **ROASTE**.

9 **IF YOU MUST** pinche somethinge in this **KYTCHEN PINCHIE the COOKE!**

10 this is my kitchen if you don't believe if **START SOMETHING**.

Leaving the kitchen, the visitor is led across to the smaller log cabin. A screen door opens on to living quarters furnished in early American style with replicas of Jesse James and Sam and Belle Star

'Wanted' posters from the Wild West decorating its rough-hewn walls. To the right of the door, in front of a picture window overlooking the highway and hills, a stone well provides cold spring water. Across the room, a large fireplace; to the left, a brass double bed in the corner. In the center of the room, behind a small wooden table and gas lamp, two rocking chairs suitable for late night reading sit next to a Franklin stove.

This is the cabin in which Muhammad Ali lives while he is training. For months he leads a Spartan existence – rising at 5:00 a.m. and ringing the bell to wake his eleven man crew. Breakfast is at eight, followed by a four mile run through the woods and fields, a workout in the gym before lunch at 1:00 p.m. Then a nap followed by business and conversation until 3:30, when he dons his sweatsuit and heads to the gym for another workout or sparring session. Supper is at 6:00, and sometimes he screens a video film of one of his fights in the evening, before lights out at 11:00. Lights out, that is, for the rest of the camp. For at eleven o'clock in the middle of the hills, with a gas lamp propped by his elbow, Muhammad Ali sits alone, reading, writing, studying, preparing his thoughts for the future.

THE POETRY OF
MUHAMMAD ALI

THE POETRY OF
MUHAMMAD ALI

One spring morning at eleven o'clock, I was standing in front of the kitchen, waiting for Ali to appear from the gym where he was taking a shower after his five mile morning run. Suddenly the screen door to the gym swung open with a creak, we turned and: 'Over here fella!' Ali called out and ducked back inside the cabin, leaving the door ajar. I ran across the courtyard and stepped through the door.

Ali was standing naked in the entrance to the shower, drying himself off with a small bath towel. He wasn't as tall as I had expected, but the nakedness was startling, and after saying hello and shaking hands, I sat down on the rumpled day-bed and waited for him to get dressed.

Continuing to dry himself, Ali asked me what I wanted to talk about. I reminded him that I had called to talk about his poetry, and Ali seemed pleased by the idea. 'All these people who come to see me,' he was saying, 'they just want to hear more of the same old stuff – I'm the greatest! I'm the prettiest fighter!' He raised his arms and stood naked in the doorway with a defiant look on his face. 'But I don't want to do that anymore,' he continued, rubbing his arms slowly. 'They wanted me to be professor of poetry at Oxford. Some people don't understand it, but . . .' and his words trailed off as he looked away.

Slowly, deliberately, he began to get dressed, pulling on a pair of brown trousers, a blue velours top, and the heavy hiking boots he wears at all times while training. There was another long silence,

Ali has known some people, ranging from Malcolm X to Major Coxson of the Philadelphia 'Black Mafia', who have been assassinated. Many people dislike him, others hate him, and even more are eager to use him.

and then the telephone rang. Ali leaned across the bed and pulled the phone off the hook.

'Yeah?' he said in a low, soft voice. 'Yeah, okay. Well yeah. You do that. Okay. We'll see you. Goodbye.' This was the first of many phonecalls he was to answer personally, both when I called and when I was with him at the camp. At other times, for no apparent

"No drinking, no women, I got fresh air up here, fresh water, vegetables, you can breathe ..."

reason, he would refuse to come to the phone. This, coupled with the fact that there were never any bodyguards evident at the camp, surprised me. Ali has known some people, ranging from Malcolm X to Major Coxson of the Philadelphia 'Black Mafia', who have been assassinated. Many people dislike him, others hate him, and even more are eager to use him. He receives a constant stream of requests for interviews and endorsements of every kind. Still, he often answers his own telephone and always leaves his doors unlocked.

Ali swung his legs back over the day-bed and stood up. 'Let me put this thing away,' he said, pointing down toward the bed. I got up and watched him fold the brown army blanket carefully before placing the bed against the wall. Then he sat in a straight-backed chair beside the door leading out to the gym.

For a full minute I waited for him to speak, watching him, but he was staring at the floor, distracted, as if I wasn't even in his room. Finally he slid his right hand up under his shirt, pulling the shirt up and revealing a layer of fat around his waist. He looked up and caught me staring at him. 'Gotta lose this,' he said, rubbing his stomach in a circular motion, staring back at the floor. 'No drinking, no women, I got fresh air up here, fresh water, vegetables, you can breathe . . .

'Gotta lose this,' he said again, standing up and walking toward the door. 'Come on, we'll go over to the kitchen.' I followed him into the courtyard. As he strode ahead, he suddenly stopped, his fists at waist level, danced three steps, threw a quick punch into the air, and settled back into a walk again. I followed him into the kitchen.

'See that sign?' he asked, stopping in the center of the cafeteria and pointing to the far wall. 'My father painted it. He's painted all the signs up here.' He crossed to the coffee machines: 'Help yourself,' he said, without turning around.

I took a seat at one of the long tables, and Ali began talking about the origins of his poetry.

'It was '62, when I fought Archie Moore. Moore rhymed with four, so the publicity for that fight was:

Moore will
hit the floor
in round four

Then I fought Henry Cooper, I said:
This is no jive
Cooper will
leave in five

One thing led to another.' As the conversation progressed, Ali became increasingly absorbed, rocking back and forth in his metal chair, bringing his fist down on the table to establish a point, laughing, smiling, frowning in mock ferocity as he read his fight poems. Then suddenly he switched off, slowed down and, gazing past me, explained: 'But I don't write these boxing poems much anymore. Sometimes I write poems now, but they're different. I just wrote a freedom poem, goes like this:

Freedom

Better far, from all I see,
To die fighting to be free.
What more fitting end could be?

Better surely than in some bed,
Where in broken health I'm led,
Lingering until I'm dead.

Better than with cries and pleas
Or in the clutch of some disease,
Wastin' slowly by degrees.
Better than of heart attack
Or some dose of drug I lack,
Let me die by being black.

Better far that I should go
Standing here against the foe.
Is there sweeter death to know?
Better than the bloody stain
On some highway where I'm lain,
Torn by flyin' glass and pain.

Better call on death to come
Than to die another dumb
Looted victim in the slum.

Better than of prison rot,
If there's any choice I've got,
Rather perish on the spot.

Better now my fight to wage,
Now while my blood boils with rage,
Less it cool with ancient age.

Better valid for me to die
Than to Uncle Tom and try
Making peace just to live a lie.

Better if I say my sooth,
I'm gonna die demandin' truth
While I'm still akin to youth.

Better now than later on,
Now that the fear of death is gone,
Never mind another dawn.

'Bad!' he swore softly, looking across at me. He had been reciting from memory. 'These are some of the things I don't reveal to the public too much. Here's another. This poem is entitled "Truth":

Truth

The face of truth is open
The eyes of truth are bright
The lips of truth are never closed
The head of truth is upright.

The breath of truth stands forward
The gaze of truth is straight
Truth has neither fear nor doubt
Truth has patience to wait.

The words of truth are touching
The voice of truth is deep
The law of truth is simple
All that you sew you reap.

The soul of truth is flaming
The heart of truth is warring
The mind of truth is clear
And firm through rain and storm.

Facts are but its shadow
Truth stands above all sin
Great be the battle of life
Truth in the end shall win.

The image of truth is Elijah Muhammad
Wisdom's message his rod
The sign of truth is the crescent
The soul of truth is God.

The life of truth is eternal
Immortal is its past
Truth has the power to endure
Truth shall always last.

'That's my masterpiece,' he said, and slumped back in his chair.
After a couple of minutes – during which Ali rubbed his
stomach and looked out of the window – I asked him how he
found the time to write. 'During the night sometimes,' he said.

THE ART OF
PERSONALITY

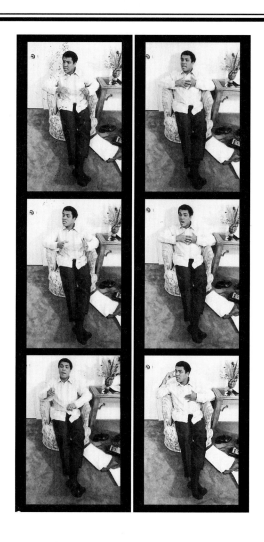

THE ART OF
PERSONALITY

wondered how he managed to train on three hours sleep: 'Do you often stay up that late?' 'Sometimes I do. What happens is, when I'm in the city and I'm eating cheeseburgers and drinking sodas and I'm up all night, I can't think. See, I wrote a thing once:

Those living close to nature
In solitude as peasants in the country,
Have a greater intuition
Than educated people living the city life.

Why?' He sat forward, taking a deep breath. 'I'm breathing fresh air, my mind is clear. You're not, in New York City. I'm drinking fresh water from the ground, rain water; there's nothing in it. You can taste that water when you drink it. The food that I eat, the vegetables are not frozen or sprayed. There's a farm down the road. The tomatoes I eat, the lady picks them out of her garden. So I'm nourishing in my soul and my thoughts real water and real food, which is the nature for the body. So I seem better than the man who's eating artificial food, breathing artificial air. This is one of the things that gives me the incentive to keep going, having this place. You know, if I was still in a hotel or in somebody's gym, I'd be bored. And now this, this is like real life. Fresh air, fresh water, peace, looking at the view: can't beat it. I didn't know it would be this nice. I'm predicting there's not a camp in the world **34** like this one for boxing. I mean, you talk about training and going

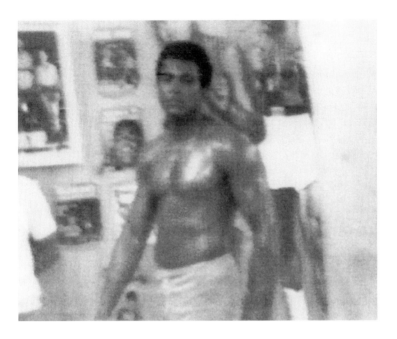

to camp, you think about chopping wood and walking up hills and sledding. And that's just what this is, horses and . . .'

'You ride the horses?' I broke in.

'Yeah! I ride em, man. I can ride like Roy Rogers! Can I ride? You stick around a little while, you gonna see me ride!

'They say wise men go off and meditate on top of a mountain, and fast and think. They just eat honey and no vegetables and no meat, and things just come to them. I wrote something the other day:

"I'm breathing fresh air, my mind is clear. You're not, in New York City. I'm drinking fresh water from the ground, rain water; there's nothing in it. You can taste that water when you drink it. The food that I eat, the vegetables are not frozen or sprayed."

The world is a field,
And we are born to cultivate the field.
Once we learn to cultivate the field,
We can produce anything.

'So you see, I can sit down and figure out a problem. I know the nature of different races. I know what to say and what not to say. I put it all together, and I can use it.

The man who has no imagination
Stands on the earth.
He has no wings,
He cannot fly.'

Ali begins to sound like a preacher, his voice turning soft, melodious and emphatic with measured breath as he speaks in a mixture of rhyme and reason. He repeats the last poem, one of his most frequent central statements, slowly, making it clear and strong:

The man who has no imagination
Stands on the earth.

Looking up, almost in a whisper:

He has no wings,
He cannot fly.

He begins parodying himself, letting his eyes bug out, large and round: 'Joe Frazier has no imagination! George Foreman has no imagination!' He lifts his finger to the end of his nose and

"Joe Frazier has no imagination! George Foreman has no imagination! They just pugnosed boxers! Left hook here, right hook there, and that don't attract the women who like ice skaters."

"You talk jive, you'll fall in five. That won't do, you go in two. I'm the greatest! Hiya, haha! I'll get them there."

squashes it against his face. 'They just pugnosed boxers! Left hook here, right hook there, and that don't attract the women who like ice skaters. That don't attract the fan who likes to play bridge. That don't attract the man in Africa or England. But my image and my imagination does. But boxers – they just draw the boxing fans.'

He pauses, slouching into his chair, the perfect ham actor. With little gestures of hand and face, he becomes an old man with a hat and a cigar: 'There's an old fellow sitting there with his head down and a cigar.' Ali's voice becomes thick and monotonous: 'Joe! Come on yum hum hum yaha!' He sits straight up in his chair, slamming the top of the table. 'That ain't colorful! But I come on in my pretty white robe, do my shuffle!' His feet dance under the table as he turns from side to side. 'And my predictions!' He starts to wave his arms around again, rolls his eyes and sounds a little hysterical as he acts out the part of Muhammad Ali, boxer: 'You

37

talk jive, you'll fall in five. That won't do, you go in two. I'm the greatest! Hiya, haha! I'll get them there.'

Then he becomes the fight fan, a young man in bow tie and madras jacket, with a blonde on his arm: '"Hey! Let's get a ticket, go and see this!" You gotta laugh it up, make it colorful.'

Suddenly Ali sits back in his chair, looks up calmly, and says, conclusively: 'Imagination. See, I fly. They stand still. See, I got this lecture, The Power of Suggestion. I suggest to myself that I'm going to do this and do that, and I do it. I believe I'm gonna get him in this round; I practise it. And I believe I can do this, and do it. Confidence. Confidence. Every man wants to be determined. Every man wants to believe in himself, every man wants to be fearless. And when I display this, it attracts people; they come to see if I can do it.

> **"Confidence. Confidence. Every man wants to be determined. Every man wants to believe in himself, every man wants to be fearless."**

"'I'm beautiful! I'm too pretty to be a fighter! Look at me! I'm the prettiest fighter! There ain't never been a fighter so beautiful! And they just say, 'He's crazy!'"

Many of them envy you, because they want to do it, and they can't. Many of them like it; many of them don't like it. Many like you for it. See?'

'Do you have any other lectures?' I ask.

'Yeah,' he replies. 'I studied a few things, putting topics together. I just spoke to Cornell College, spoke on the topic of friendship. I'm getting lectures together before I even know where I'm speaking. Lectures on different subjects. I carry a briefcase of them, and when I go to a lot of places, a lot of times I don't know what type of college it is. After sitting down and weighing out the situation, I pull out a lecture to fit the occasion.

'I have another lecture called "The Art of Personality." And the lecture says: personality's not something you're born with; we're

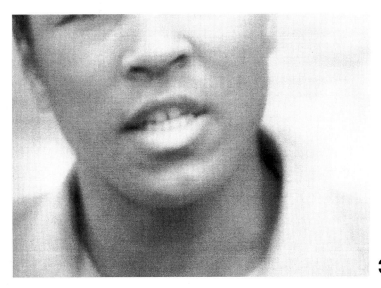

"Then I attract the black militants that don't like the whites: "Yeah! Tell 'em brother. Tell them honkies, brother!"

born as individuals. My wife's got four children and all of them have got different individualities. So what I'm saying is, personality is the development of individuality.

'Take me for example. I attract people. Pretty girls from all over the country charter planes to my fights because I say things that attract them: "I'm beautiful! I'm too pretty to be a fighter! Look at me! I'm the prettiest fighter! There ain't never been a fighter so beautiful! And they just say "He's crazy!" They know I'm pretty.' Ali is beginning to enjoy himself. Grinning broadly, he acts out the role of each person.

'Then I attract the

redneck white folks that don't like black people: "I'm the greatest!"' he yells, rolling his eyes with his fist in front of his face. "'That nigger's too arrogant; he talks too much!"' Ali says in a tight, angry, dull voice.

'I'm pretty! I can't lose! I'm the greatest!' he yells again.

'The nigger needs a whoppin'!'

'Then I attract the black militants that don't like the whites: "Yeah! Tell 'em brother. Tell them honkies, brother!"'

'Then I got all the long-haired hippies, because I don't go to war. I ain't goin' to no Vietnam. I say:

Clean out my cell
And take my tail
On the trail
For the jail
Without bail

Because it's better in jail
Watchin' television fed
Than in Vietnam somewhere dead.

'Then I attract the Muslims, because of the name Muhammad Ali. Then the Israeli, who don't get along with the Muslims, might come to see me get whupped, because I'm a Muslim. And the Muslim's gonna root for me, because he don't want the Israeli to get his wishes. So you add it all up, I got a helluva crowd. Personality.' He sits back, looking confident and amused.

'So is that why you're successful?' I ask. He shoots me one of those Muhammad Ali fierce looks.

'Why are you successful?' I ask, still laughing.

"Many things could be accomplished if we only believed. I was determined that I would be successful. I thought about it, I dreamed about it, I slept it, I ate it . . . and I believed."

Ali grows serious again, speaking softly and evenly.

'I would say determination to be successful in whatever field you endeavor. Then hope, in whatever field you determine to be successful. Hope comes from the determination to achieve something. So therefore, this determination in itself can be a very great power. The goal which a person determines to reach is small in comparison to the power that he gains in the process of determination. And in itself, belief is another thing which a lot of men don't have, belief. Many things could be accomplished if we only believed. I was determined that I would be successful. I thought about it, I dreamed about it, I slept it, I ate it . . . and I believed. Number One is Allah, A-L-L-A-H, God is the number one reason to whom I give credit for my success. Allah, the strong belief in Allah. I have a poem:

Life is a fair trade where all adjusts itself in time.
For all that you take from it, you must pay the price sooner or later.
For some things, you must pay in advance.
For some things, you must pay on delivery.
And for others, later on, when the bill is presented.'

He read some other poems, commenting on them as he went along:

Where is a man's wealth? His wealth is in his knowledge.
If his wealth is in the bank, and not in his knowledge,
Then he doesn't possess it, because it's in the bank.

'Ain't that beautiful? A man with no money can get it. They had me broke at one time. I was fighting and thinking and writing, and I came back. A lot of people lose their money; but with no mind they don't get it again.' Ali read the poem a second time, putting a gentle emphasis on 'because it's in the bank.'

Do not weep with the sad, but console them.
If not, by your tears,
You will only water the plant of their sorrow.

'The lady's crying,' Ali screws his face into a tight knot of tears and wails in a high-pitched voice: 'Oh mah son is dead! Ohhh hoo hoo oh I'm so sorry! Ooooh oooh they gonna bury him tomorrow! They gonna bury him! Oh they are! Ooooh ooh ooh ooh.' He is rocking back and forth in his chair. Then suddenly he stops, straightening up and smiling: 'See, that's not helping her,' he says. 'Do not weep with the sad, but console them. If not, by your tears, you only water the plant of their sorrow.'

"I'm visiting a prison tomorrow; Rubin Hurricane Carter, a great fighter, is in prison. Many people say he's innocent; from what I heard, he's innocent."

He pauses for a moment, then looks down at his handwritten manuscripts for the next poem.

Life is a continuing battle,
And he alone is victorious who conquers himself.

'What moved me to write that?' he asks. 'See, when I'm up here in training and I have to dodge women, I have to dodge certain types of food, it's a constant battle. But if I can fight myself, defeat myself, I'll go right through it. And I don't care what race you are, what religion or what country. This is true facts of everybody's nature,' he adds.

'I'm visiting a prison tomorrow; Rubin Hurricane Carter, a great fighter, is in prison. Many people say he's innocent; from what I heard, he's innocent.'

'What's he in jail for?' I interrupt, remembering something

43

about Carter's case.

'I don't know,' Ali says. 'Manslaughter or something. They don't know who did it, and he was in the car.'

'Yeah. He's been in for a long time, hasn't he?'

'Yeah. So I'm supposed to go – somebody invited me – and there are a couple of hard wardens on him there, so I wrote this:

> The warden of the prison is in worse condition than the prisoner himself.
> While the body of the prisoner is in captivity,
> The mind of the warden is in prison.'

'Better not read that in prison,' I tell him, but Ali is already looking down at his next poem.

Since he refused his induction to Vietnam and changed his name from Cassius Clay to Muhammad Ali, declaring support for Elijah Muhammad and the Black Muslim movement, Ali has emerged as a man with a message. And it is not about boxing; he really didn't want to talk about that any more. Whenever I brought it up, he steered the conversation back to what he now considers his major tasks: writing, running the camp, thinking. Boxing was a metaphor, a chest of tools into which he could reach for illustrations, something in which he was expert, but disinterested.

I asked him if he believed in inspiration. 'Yeah. Inspiration is just somebody who inspires you, like our religious leader in America, Elijah Muhammad. He's been here forty-two years trying to unite black people, clean 'em up, give 'em work, teach 'em to do for themselves, quit begging white people, get out and work, respect your woman. And he's running a whole nation from his living room. And one man doing all that inspires me to say: "Well, he runs a whole nation of people, so I can watch this camp, I can make sure they clean that bunkhouse." 'If this man seventy-five years old can handle a whole nation with all those black people, then I can handle my little world, from my house to my camp to my office.'

MUHAMMAD'S
MOUNTAIN

MUHAMMAD'S MOUNTAIN

Following the example of Elijah Muhammad, Ali runs his house, camp, and office with a combination of discipline, respect, and good humour. His wife Belinda, the austere mother of Ali's three young daughters and infant son, spends most of her time in their $250,000 Spanish-style home in the fashionable suburb of Cherry Hill, New Jersey, looking after the education of her children, whom she is preparing for formal Muslim schools in Chicago.

One afternoon, as I am sitting with Ali on half a tree trunk converted into a bench in the courtyard, Belinda emerges from the cabin. She is tall, about 5 feet 11, and fairly slim, and always wears long dresses or skirts that reach her ankles. She often wears sunglasses. Today she is followed by a demure elderly nurse in a white uniform who is leading the children along. As Belinda looks on, the nurse brings little Muhammad over, and his father picks him up. 'Don't he look like me?' Ali asks, beaming. He kisses and hugs the child, who sits happily for a few minutes, cradled in his father's massive arms. Then he squirms down on to the bench and waddles away. Ali watches proudly as the nurse leads Muhammad back to join his sisters.

Later, Belinda shows some tourists around the camp. Dressed in a long white skirt, she escorts a group of children through the gym and across to Coretta's kitchen, explaining that Coretta is Ali's aunt. She laughs at their jokes, smiles constantly, and is a model guide, but maintains a certain distance.

46 For the past two years, Ali has spent most of his time training

for fights at camp, or traveling to fulfill various engagements. Though he spends little time in Cherry Hill with his family, they occasionally visit the camp for a week at a time, and, with his children around him, Ali quickly falls into the role of educator and disciplinarian. 'I wrote something the other day,' he says, turning back to us: 'Do not take an example of another as an excuse for your own wrongdoing. Right? My little daughter Jamillah did something that caused me to write this. She said, "Well,

Without breaking stride, Ali scoops her up in his arms, shouting, 'Look at that pretty girl! What are you doing today? How do you feel?' He hugs her, kisses her, and puts her back on the ground. She smiles up at him.

47

Reeshemah did it. "Why?" I said, "Well, Reeshemah was wrong. You can't be wrong because she was wrong.'"

But as with everything else he does, Ali balances this discipline with plenty of good-natured spontaneity. Later, as we're walking past the gym, we see Reeshemah talking with a group of other children. Without breaking stride, Ali scoops her up in his arms, shouting, 'Look at that pretty girl! What are you doing today? How do you feel?' He hugs her, kisses her, and puts her back on the ground. She smiles up at him.

In camp, the people closest to Ali are cornerman and court jester Bundini Brown; Angelo Dundee, his trainer; Blood, his second cornerman; and Gene Kilroy, who looks after his practical daily affairs. Again following the example of Elijah Muhammad, Ali is very much in charge of his entourage and, though no one is put into the position of being a 'yes' man, everyone is subjected to Ali's rigorous discipline at one time or another. He has a poem that goes:

Destiny
Destiny can take your best friend
As an instrument to cause you harm
And your worst enemy to do you good.

Reading it, he adds: 'Right? Judas betrayed Jesus, and Malcolm X betrayed Elijah Muhammad. I just fired two fellers who were with me for a few years. Then there are some people who didn't used to like me; now they say: "You know, I been watching you. I like you now." One time I couldn't fight in this country. One time I couldn't box nowhere. Now they beg me to come. T.V. nation-wide shows. They name fights after me. Destiny caused this, see? Isn't that beautiful?'

Bundini, Angelo, Blood and Gene respect Ali with an emotional loyalty no argument can crack. They have stuck together for a long time, through many trials, and they would not have stayed on if anything else meant more to them. At camp, they live together in the fourth cabin, dug into the hill above the

courtyard.

Bundini Brown saunters around the corner of the gym and heads across the courtyard wearing a Hawaiian shirt and tight small red woolen cap, his thin legs clad in yellow cotton trousers. He moves with the authority of a man who is used to being watched. Suddenly Blood steps quietly out from the shadows of the kitchen wall and says something under his breath.

'What you say?' Bundini snaps, tensing just noticeably under the graceful swagger.

'When you live on the hill, you live by the rules of the hill,' Blood snarls. 'You were in later than eleven last night.'

Bundini turns around quickly and walks off up the hill, muttering to himself; Blood follows him resentfully with his eyes. Ten minutes later, Bundini emerges from the cabin with a sheaf of papers in his hand, talking to a young aide; they walk slowly down the hill. Halfway down, Bundini stops, wags his finger angrily at the young man, then turns and walks back uphill quickly, glancing over his shoulder with a threatening look to make sure that he will be obeyed. The aide stares helplessly at the ground.

Other things mark Bundini. As Ali's court jester and cornerman,

Bundini appeared as the Black Mafia's right hand killer in 'Shaft' and 'Shaft's Big Score'. 'I didn't get a chance to show my dimples, though, see? That's the only thing I didn't like about it,' he says.

he works hard at both jobs and has been irreplaceable. His casual style reminds you that the regimentation of camp life has its necessary exceptions. Outside camp, Bundini keeps himself busy by devoting his considerable talents and energy to such diverse activities as writing (he is currently working on a book called *Only Human*, which is, he says, 'about people . . . on this planet'), travel, and films (he appeared as the Black Mafia's right hand killer in 'Shaft' and 'Shaft's Big Score.' 'I didn't get a chance to show my dimples, though, see? That's the only thing I didn't like about it,' he says).

I'm lounging around the gym, talking with a television crew, when Bundini angles in, smiling behind a pair of thick brown-framed glasses, to start a game of craps. Soon the dice are rattling

51

to the rhythm of Bundini's hypnotic calls. The T.V. director has lost fifty dollars in ten minutes and tries to back out, but Bundini moves fast, calling three more bets before the director can take his hand out of his pocket. Next Bundini wants me to play, but I start asking questions instead. He says he won't give me an interview unless I pay him. Offering him supper instead, I keep telling him how great I think he is.

'Supper?' exclaims an incredulous Mr. Brown, slapping his ample stomach with one thin hand and staring at me with calm, cocksure eyes: 'Baby, you know I ain't hungry. What you want to talk about?'

> **"Paid my rent when I was nine – bop de bop bop bam bam – born on a doorstep with no cross or chair, had to suck the first nipple that came along – bop de bop bop bam bam – never had a diaper service, been around the world twenty-six times . . ."** Bundini Brown

'What do you do all the time up here?' I begin, countering his gaze by hopping from foot to foot. He shifts his attention to a small punching bag just to the right of his head, and begins swatting it rhythmically as we walk.

'What do I do day by day? (Bop de bop bop bam bam goes the punching.)

'Yeah.'

'Be a friend,' he replies.

'What's your reputation based on?'

'Paid my rent when I was nine – bop de bop bop bam bam – born on a doorstep with no cross or chair, had to suck the first nipple that came along – bop de bop bop bam bam – never had a diaper service, been around the world twenty-six times . . .'

'What were you doing before you were with Ali?'

'I was with Sugar Ray Robinson for nine years,' Bundini says, dropping his hands. 'He was something like Ali. Great religious type of thing.'

'How would you describe Ali to someone who had never met him?'

The answer came back fast and hard: 'That he's a prophet.'

'How about personally, though?'

'Like a little boy. Find a little boy in a person, you find common sense. Find common sense, you find equal justice among people.'

(Earlier that day, I had been sitting opposite Ali in the kitchen, watching him write a lecture. Bundini was sitting at the corner of the table, reading a magazine. As he finished each sheet of paper, Ali would hand it to me. Occasionally he'd look up, saying, 'Isn't this beautiful?' and read a page he'd just written. Bundini would put his magazine down and – with his chin in his hands,

leaning toward Ali – drink in every word.)

'What did you feel like when Ali read those things this morning?' I ask. 'Were you moved by it?'

'I get moved by the things that I like; some things I don't get moved by. What I like, he moves me more than the average person do . . .' Bundini pauses, gazing straight at me. 'Otherwise we

53

wouldn't be together. God put us together; I didn't get my job from the employment office.'

I throw some more questions at Bundini. Finally he says, 'You don't know anything about me, do you?'

'Oh yeah, I do,' I protest. 'I know you have a good sense of humour, you're not boring.'

'Right. But I do all that crying all the time. Don't that mess you up? Why do I cry?'

A door swings open to our right, interrupting the conversation, and Angelo Dundee steps up to have a word with Bundini.

Dundee – a short, inconspicuously dressed man with a reddish toupee and glasses – has been Ali's trainer for over ten years. He is a soft-spoken, friendly man who seems to be least involved with Ali's intellectual life, most involved with his training and boxing. His habitual relationship with Ali, tested by many conflicts they've withstood together, has developed into a deep trust and easy-going exchange. They move comfortably in and out of each other's orbits, and if Angelo sets the guidelines for training, he also knows Ali's judgement is as good as his own most of the time.

After lunch one afternoon, as we're inspecting the rocks with Ali, Dundee passes by. 'You gonna lie down, Muhammad?' he asks.

'No, not today.'

'Okay,' Angelo replies, without a hint of protest. Ali grins and calls after him, 'I can't do much layin' down today, you hear?'

Dundee's view of Ali is completely positive but slightly distanced by a managerial concern over what Ali will do next. Thus when Ali had first suggested the idea of the camp, Angelo

"You gonna lie down, Muhammad?" he asks. "No, not today." "Okay," Angelo replies, without a hint of protest. Ali grins and calls after him, "I can't do much layin' down today, you hear?"

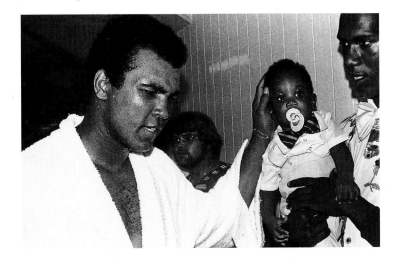

had argued against it.

'You know, I didn't think he'd stick to it,' he tells me, carefully drawing a pipe out of his mouth and gazing at it. 'I've seen him pick up so many things with total enthusiasm, only to drop them six months later. I was worried he was going to spend a lot of money on this place and lose interest half way through. And once Muhammad's lost interest, there's nothing you can do about it.' He pauses for a minute to light his pipe. 'Anyway, Ali didn't drop it. He's stuck to it, and it's already paid off the $200,000 invested. See, when he used to train in Florida his hotel bills were $10,000 a month easy, what with three meals a day and all the rooms and suites he had to rent. He realised he could build himself a log cabin for $10,000. Also he wanted the country air, fresh food and hills to run through. He's got it all here, and it's working out fine.'

Angelo is obviously pleased with the camp now, in all its aspects. He is the picture of total dedication – sweeping the gymnasium floor, supervising odd jobs, handling many routine aspects of Ali's public relations – always with the same concern that the job be done right and on time. Unlike Bundini and Blood, he rarely sits around making smalltalk.

I'm sitting in the kitchen with Ali and Bundini, talking about a lecture Ali is writing called 'The Education of the Infant'. 'The cake sprouted from a hot plate with some grease on it,' Bundini is saying. 'You take sugar, eggs, powder, all kinds of things, and when it's over, it's one sight and one flavor. You're looking at a person!'

Ali chuckles. Angelo comes through the door. 'Is Wednesday okay for the press to come down?' he asks loudly, interrupting to get Ali's attention. Ali thinks for a minute: 'Wednesday's fine,' he says, chuckling again and turning back to the conversation. 'You sure now?' says Angelo, concerned, walking over beside Ali and placing one hand on the back of his chair. 'Yeah,' Ali says, with a touch of impatience. 'Wednesday's fine.' 'Okay, you got it! You got it!' sings the ebullient Angelo, walking around the room, straightening a couple of chairs. There is a large 'No Smoking' sign in the kitchen, and he has left the perennial pipe outside. 'Wednesday it is!' he concludes, heading for the door with another

pipe already in his hand.

But if Angelo sometimes seems to create work for its own sake, he too is kept in line by Ali's firm control over the camp, and is not above taking orders. We're standing outside by the edge of Ali's cabin, talking, when Ali suddenly gets an idea. 'Hey Angelo!' he calls out, without turning around. Dundee is twenty yards behind him, watering some trash with a garden hose, and doesn't respond. 'Angelo!' Ali calls out again, but Dundee still doesn't hear him. Ali whirls around, angry: 'Angelo, come over here!' he snaps. Dundee looks up, startled, drops the hose, and trots over with a look of deep concern.

Blood keeps a lower profile around the camp than do Angelo or **57**

Bundini. He is a retired boxer, and it seems that his respect for Ali is due more to Ali's physical prowess and professional accomplishments than to his intellectual efforts.

Between training sessions, when he stands by with a stopwatch in hand or rubs Ali's back and arms with oil, Blood is primarily in charge of seeing that the physical labor around the camp gets done. He presides over a series of jobs with slow, steady thoroughness, only occasionally seeming to betray a touch of insecurity about his role in the group. He enjoys talking to the various sparring partners who regularly appear at the camp, and presides as a dry foil to Bundini's caustic wit over the dinner table. As he and Bundini go at it from opposite ends of the table one night, a strange, slightly nervous silence holds the room:

'Look at Blood go! That nigger's got a hunger!' Bundini cracks.

Blood puts a chicken bone down on his plate, sits back deliberately and: 'Your mouth's so full of nonsense, Bundini, you don't have room for a meal,' he says, arching one eyebrow. Bundini grins.

'You aren't from Crawdaddy, are you?' he asks a young reporter one day. 'Because they wrote a really nasty piece...Talked about the way Ali treated his white lackeys and stuff,' Gene says, upset.

Blood is clearly, after Bundini himself, the most hard-headed person there, the best friend and worst enemy. He inspires total confidence with his quiet professionalism, his iron strong, slim body and still face. It is easy to see why Ali has him in his corner.

Gene does not quite share the substantially black humor that holds the crew together during the tough months of training, and though he gets along well with everyone, he seems to prefer to sit alone, going over events, answering phones, always worrying.

'You aren't from Crawdaddy, are you?' he asks a young reporter one day. 'Because they wrote a really nasty piece.'

'No, I'm not,' the reporter says. 'What did they say?'

'Talked about the way Ali treated his white lackeys and stuff,' Gene says, upset. Obviously he feels that he has been singled out as the white lackey. He isn't. 'I've been with Ali twelve years unofficially; four years officially,' Gene says. 'I feel like a brother to him. This thing wouldn't end unless Ali said, "So long."'

Gene is always busy at Ali's side in public events around the country. When you see two men holding Ali back in a television studio as he shouts at George Foreman, tearing his jacket off, ready to brawl, the tall white man with thick black curly hair and moustache is Gene. The other man is Ali's slightly younger brother, Rahmann, also a Muslim, who works full time at the

59

camp as a senior aide and is often quietly at Ali's side.

Ali expects and gets a high performance from every person he employs. He gets it more because they respect him than because he tells them he wants it, but he isn't remiss at telling people off. We're sitting in the kitchen; Ali is writing at one of the tables. Gene comes in with a sheaf of bills in his hand and, crouching down by Ali's chair, asks him to sign a couple of checks. Ali looks over the bills and, without raising his voice, but with a touch of anger so that he talks faster, snaps: 'I never ordered those fences. There you go again. I told you: don't go spending my money without asking me first.'

'But I didn't, Ali!' Gene protests. He looks up, worried, but

If anyone from outside the camp criticizes a friend, Ali is quick to come to the defense. 'I got a saying: Blessed are they who cover the scars of others, even from their own eyes. You've got a fault, and the word's getting out,' he explains. 'They say: "You know him. What is it?" I say: "It's a damn lie. He's not that way."

there is no room for protest. Ali is already writing again.

On the other hand, if arguments arise in camp, and if Gene or Angelo gets told off, it's because Ali feels that it's his duty, and his alone, to run the camp as he would his own home – in all its aspects, following the example of Elijah Muhammad.

It's not a matter of any lack of respect. If anyone from outside the camp criticizes a friend, Ali is quick to come to the defense. 'I got a saying: Blessed are they who cover the scars of others, even from their own eyes. You've got a fault, and the word's getting out,' he explains. 'They say: "You know him. What is it?" I say: "It's a damn lie. He's not that way." And yet you are that way, but I'm going to cover you from him. Now I'm trying to forgive you; I'm going along with you. I don't want to say . . . See?'

Ali's relationships with people outside his circle, ranging from the most casual visitor to what he might call his 'office' relationships, is another matter altogether. He is rarely, if ever, critical or demanding: quite the opposite. Day after day he will perform tirelessly for visitors – ranging from Elvis Presley and Sammy Davis Jr. to faded Hollywood stars, boy scouts and itinerant hippies – with an inexhaustible good humor.

We're standing in front of the camp with Ali and Gene. A small group of tourists hovers ten feet away. They've come to see the Champ. Ali never ignores them. Today he is sparring with a nine-year-old blond boy, and he pretends to be knocked down. The toupeed father from New Jersey ecstatically films the fight with a **61**

small Bolex. As he finishes, Ali takes the youngster by the shoulders and tells him: 'Now you can tell all your friends that you fought Muhammad Ali and knocked him down. That'll make you famous!' He runs into the gym and returns carrying Floyd Patterson's golden gloves, to show them to the kids.

Another time we're again standing by the rock in front of the camp, and Gene comes over, followed by a thin, long-haired hippie. 'Listen Muhammad, here's a friend of mine,' Gene says.

'Yeeeeeeeaaaahh?' Ali exclaims, bursting into a big smile and laughing as he shakes hands with the young man.

'He just packed up and left home,' Gene says, egging Ali on.

Ali gets right into the swing of the situation: 'You did the right thing! You did the right thing!'

'You got to be a hippie to make it,' the hippie replies.

'You don't wear no shoes?' Ali asks, pointing to the hippie's bare feet.

'Did till they wore out.'

Ali laughs again. 'How many clothes you carry with you?'

'Muh jeans, pants, pair of shorts, couple of shirts.'

'That's all, huh?' Ali asks, acting incredulous.

'Toothbrush,' the hippie adds.

'No kidding. You're not married? You don't worry about nobody?'

The hippie draws himself up. 'I been through them things,' he says proudly.

'You walk the highway barefoot?' Ali asks. 'You got some shoes, don't you?'

'I got a pair of flip-flops for the rocky roads.'

'Yeah? How old are you then?'

'Twenty-six. You get used to it, you know.'

'Yeah,' says Ali, shaking hands as the hippie moves on. Later, he turns to us: 'You gotta admire somebody like that,' he says.

Perhaps the most vivid example I saw of an 'office' or 'business' relationship was that of Ali and one Harvey Moyer. A certain morning, I came into the gym to find Ali surrounded by eight children – his own and some of the retainers'. They were jumping all over him, running up and down. He was shouting and playing. He waved as I drifted past and took a seat against the wall beside a punching bag. Bundini, Angelo, Blood, Rahmann, Gene, and six younger aides were all there, joking with Ali, relaxing.

'Come over to the kitchen in about an hour,' Ali called out. 'Someone I want you to meet.'

An hour later, I'm walking toward the kitchen. A sedan pulls up nearby and a short, puffy, round white man pulls himself out from behind the wheel. His watery eyes look around anxiously.

The kitchen door opens. Ali leans out and yells, 'Hey Harvey! Come on in!' Then he looks at me, winks, and tells me to come in too.

Harvey reaches the kitchen door out of breath. 'I . . . know you're busy,' he pants to Ali. 'I . . . just came up . . . to look at the bell.'

'Come on in! Come on in!' Ali insists, leading us all toward a table. He produces some coffee, and we sit down.

Looking across at me seriously, Ali breaks the silence. 'A new angle. Now very seriously get this,' he begins. 'You got your tape on?'

'Yeah,' I admit.

'Okay. I want you to meet Mr. Moyer. How do you spell it?'

'M-O-Y-E-R.' Moyer jerks the letters out, still breathless. I look at him, wondering who he is, why he deserves this big presentation. 'Moyer?' I ask.

'See my bell outside?' Ali asks enthusiastically, pointing at Moyer. 'He bought that bell for hisself. And he gave me the bell.' Ali lets that sink in, but still don't have the Moyer equation worked out.

'He paid about $3000 for the bell. He gave me the bell for $1500. The bell weighs how much?'

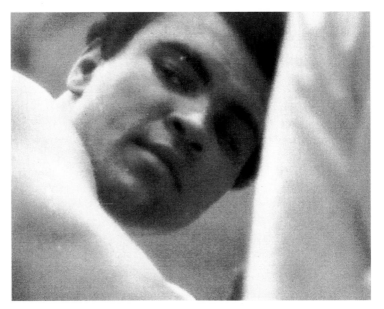

"Harvey Moyer's been the biggest thing that's happened to me since finding this ground. He brought me my rocks; it was his idea, he told me. He gave me the first rock, and he suggested putting Jack Johnson's name on it."

'Seven hundred and fifty pounds,' the 250 pound Moyer replies from behind a light gray knit shirt.

'It's very old and you can hear it all over,' Ali continues. 'And it's antique. Harvey Moyer's been the biggest thing that's happened to me since finding this ground. He brought me my rocks; it was his idea, he told me. He gave me the first rock, and he suggested putting Jack Johnson's name on it. Come on outside, let me show you. Got your camera?' The three of us get up and walk slowly around the gym toward the entranceway.

'So how long ago did you first meet Ali?' I ask Moyer.

Moyer screws up his face. 'Oh . . . er . . . um . . .'

'Two months ago,' Ali interjects.

Moyer nods slowly, thinking: 'About . . . two months.'

'So what inspired you to give him the bell, to bring the bell up here?'

Moyer stares at me as if he doesn't understand my question: 'This week er . . .'

Ali breaks in again, leaning across Moyer: 'I went looking for bells.'

'He went lookin',' Moyer says, with a resigned nod.

When we reach the rock, Ali directs the pose: 'I'll stand with my hand out, and Mr. Moyer will present this rock to me. He gave it to me. He'll hold his hand out . . .'

As soon as the appropriate photographs are taken, Ali asks Mr. Moyer to give me his card and makes me promise to send Moyer a copy of the photograph of them by the rock.

'Are you gonna have a rock with your name on it?' I ask.

'The whole mountain will be my rock!' Ali exclaims, quickly laughing. From that time on, Moyer appeared in the scenario quite regularly.

Another time, Ali took me aside and said, 'Look, here comes Harvey Moyer. Be nice to him, 'cause it's his birthday today, you hear? We're gonna have a surprise party for him later on tonight.' And there was Moyer, pulling himself out of his car, dropping in to see how construction was going on a cabin. I walked around with him, going over the grounds, checking the foundations of the cabin, looking at a covered wagon frame he'd just delivered.

Moyer never expressed anything but total admiration for Ali. Whenever I was alone with him, he spoke of Ali in quiet amazement, saying things like: 'I don't know how he manages to do it.' To him, Ali is a king whose every whim makes sense and whose wish is a command. He gives Ali priority over his many other, and in some cases larger, customers. I finally asked Moyer exactly what his business was. Ali listened in eagerly as he said, 'Well, we do almost anything at all. Demolition, putting steel

works up, fabricating, dismantling . . .'

'Dismantling big machines that take six months,' Ali added enthusiastically. 'Those big machines that dig coal. And then you take them to Florida and put them back up. And he's got cranes. You should see the cranes! He moves mountains!'

Perhaps the camp is so important to Ali that he gives its builder as much attention as a king would give the architect of his castle. It's more likely, however, that this is simply a good example of Ali's method of conducting business. He never tires of praising Moyer to anyone and everyone who will listen. In return, Moyer made sure the camp was finished quickly and contributed his considerable local and technical know-how to the project for a very reasonable price. Everyone was happy, and the job got done.

DOES IT LOOK
LIKE IT HURTS?

DOES IT LOOK LIKE IT HURTS?

Accompanying and offsetting the discipline he brings to his life and relationships, Ali has maintained and developed his spontaneous sense of humor. Without humor, human life is empty, is one of his favorite maxims. One afternoon, I'm watching television with Ali. He is spread out in a comfortable armchair, his chin resting on his chest. I am sitting on the edge of a small armchair, staring at the afternoon news. Behind the T.V. is a big metal box full of video-tape cassettes.

'Oh! You have video?' I say. 'What's on them?'

'Those are video cassettes of my fights. You wanna see one?' Ali asks.

'Sure.'

He reaches into the pile of cassettes, humming: 'Let's see . . .' he mutters.

He quickly finds the film he's looking for, plugs it into the T.V. set, and the newsman's face is replaced by Joey Bishop's. Joey is emceeing the fight in a red scarf and a loud check jacket.

'You sure you wanna see this now?' Ali asks, a little concerned.

'Are you kidding?' He seems pretty interested in seeing it himself.

The fight is with Joe Ellis in the Houston Astrodome (July 26, 1971, five months after he lost to Frazier). It's an exciting fight, and soon I'm perched on the edge of my chair. Ali sits behind me,

a little to the left. As the tension mounts, he ad libs short, funny poems to accompany the fight. Joey Bishop gets frenzied; he wants Ali to win, but Ellis is putting up a plucky fight. Ali flicks a couple of jabs past my ears.

'Tell me, does it look like it hurts?' he asks, leaning forward.

'No, because it's on television,' I say, nodding confidently. He smiles.

Just then the door opens and a battered middle-aged black man looks in. 'Hey Ali!' the man croaks. Ali gets up: 'Come in, come in,' he says, extending his hand. I try to concentrate on the fight,

'Want you to meet my new heavyweight, Ali,' he says. 'Yeah?' Ali says. They look over, appraising the boxer. The heavyweight speaks: 'Tink you ready for me, Awi?'

now in its tenth round.

'Just dropped by to check in,' the man says.

'Yeah.'

'Brought my new heavyweight, wanted to meet you,' he says.

'Yeah?' Ali asks.

'Yeah.' He drags in a young white meatface who nods at Ali and shuffles over to a corner seat. Ali seats the manager on a couch near the T.V. and explains what we're watching.

For the next couple of rounds, they make learned comments about the fight, then Ali flicks another jab back at my head. 'Want you to meet Jersey Joe Walcott,' he says, pointing toward the manager.

Suddenly the referee steps in past a dazed, dazzled Ellis, announcing Ali the winner on a T.K.O. Ali drops his hands and sighs. 'I knew I could do it,' he whispers, his shoulders slumped over in mock exhaustion.

'Wha!? . . .' I say, pulling myself from the T.V. screen.

'Naw . . . I was just kidding,' he says, laughing. The man on the couch shifts his face into a smile.

'Want you to meet my new heavyweight, Ali,' he says.

'Yeah?' Ali says.

They look over, appraising the boxer. The heavyweight speaks: 'Tink you ready for me, Awi?'

Ali looks back at the television ignoring the remark of the heavyweight, whose grin slowly fades. It is the 11th round.

'Do you remember what happened in this fight?' Ali asks us innocently. Not wanting to reveal my ignorance, I clear my throat authoritatively, squint at the set, think quickly and declare: 'Decision on points. You won.'

'Hey! You ain't so stupid as you look,' Ali beams. 'That's right.' And he sits back in his chair. Ten seconds later he lunges forward, kneeling and waving his hands in front of the T.V.; 'But today I gotta get a knockout, darn! I gotta get a knockout. Let's see if I can change it.'

73

The manager chuckles throatily: 'Well, we gotta get going Ali,' he says.

'Yeah, okay!' Ali throws over his shoulder, and the heavyweight crawls out the door. Ali is transfixed by the set. 'I can do it! I can do it! I can change it!' he coaxes. There are sixty seconds left in the fight. Somehow, I'm completely confused. It looks like Ellis is going the distance. I'm so excited I slip off the edge of my chair. Ali is thumping the rug with his fist. 'Now fall down boy! Fall down!' he yells at the T.V. set.

Suddenly the referee steps in past a dazed, dazzled Ellis, announcing Ali the winner on a T.K.O. Ali drops his hands and sighs. 'I knew I could do it,' he whispers, his shoulders slumped over in mock exhaustion. He jumps up grinning and goes back to his chair.

On the screen, Joey Bishop is wriggling through the crowd to ask Ali a couple of questions. He manages to appear at Ali's side and shoves a microphone up in his face.

'So you won again Muhammad!' he yells.

'You a clever man, Joey,' Ali says under his breath in the chair behind me.

We get up and walk over to the gym, talking about the fight. Ali pulls on a pair of tight leather practice gloves. Suddenly in mid-sentence he wheels around and sends the heavy bag arching towards the ceiling with a sharp right hook. The crack of leather on leather makes my blood freeze, and I get a clear idea of just how much it would hurt.

EVERYONE
RECOGNISES ME

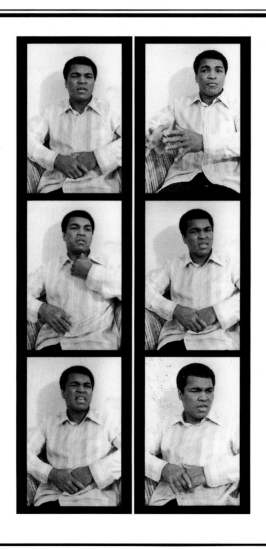

EVERYONE RECOGNISES ME

I arrive at the camp one boiling day with film-maker Anton Perich to videotape a documentary of Ali reading some of his poems. We get there a little late, and Ali is taking a nap after his morning run. Perich leaves his video-tape machine on a bench in the shade and we stroll around the camp, bumping into Angelo on the way. I introduce Anton and explain the situation. 'Well,' says Angelo, 'as long as you're waiting, why don't you come up and see the chickens we just got?' Talking graciously, he leads us up past the bunkhouse to the

chicken coop. We spend a long time looking at the chickens and listening to Angelo talk about the camp. When we get back to the bench, Perich's video equipment is no longer in the shade.

'Hey Anton,' I say, 'maybe you should move the video equipment out of the sun? It looks like it's getting a little hot.'

'No no, eez allright,' Anton says, 'zee heet does not affact.'

An hour later, Angelo tells us that Ali will be getting up soon and we should get ready. We hurry back to the video camera, eagerly talking to Anton about the first shot.

'I theenk we 'ave zee camera train on zee door when 'e come out,' Anton is saying. As we round the corner of the gym, Perich breaks into a run.

'Hey Anton! Slow down. It's . . . too hot!' I puff behind him. But then I stop. A pall of smoke hangs over the video equipment. Anton is jumping up and down on the flaming batteries which have exploded in the heat.

Anton is cursing steadily in his native Yugoslavian. 'Oh no . . .' I **77** moan. Angelo comes around the corner. 'Got your camera, he's getting . . .' Pipe half way to mouth, he stares at Anton.

'Gee, it blew up,' he says. 'It is hot up here, but see that's good for Muhammad because he's getting used to the tropical climate.'

Sweeping the remains of the video equipment into a small bag, we start running. 'Tell him – tell him – we'll be back in a couple of days . . .' we shout at Angelo, waving and jumping into our car.

A couple of days later, Anton's camera is in working order again and we return, wondering if Ali will be annoyed. He greets us warmly, making no mention of the incident, and we sit down outside to begin the interview. As the tape begins, Ali suddenly gets up and, staring down at us with his best mock-ferocious look, says:

I like your interview
And I like your style,
But your camera's so cheap
I won't talk to you for a while.

Then he storms off a few paces and comes back chuckling to begin the interview.

Ali's playfulness extends to everyone he meets. Sometimes, for no apparent reason, he will decide to cheer up everyone around him and then, when he has accomplished that, he will suddenly switch off and look away again, distracted.

One hot summer day, I was standing in the shade of the kitchen when Ali steps through the door and, noticing my overheated baleful look, motions to me with a smile: 'Come on! There's something I want you to see.'

I follow him across the courtyard to a large bus parked beside the gymnasium, and he takes me inside. It's a custom-built touring bus, compact, with a small sitting room in back, television, kitchenette, and two bedrooms on either side of a tiled bath. As I look around, Ali climbs into the driver's seat, plugs a cassette of Andy Williams into a tape deck over the windshield and, grabbing

'Do people recognize you in this area?' I ask. Ali shoots me a fierce look, and grins: 'Everyone in the world recognizes me,' he says.

the hand microphone attached to an intercom, calls out: 'On your left is Hoboken, the little lady with the shopping bag . . . Want to go for a ride?'

A few minutes later, we're racing down Highway 61, talking a mile a minute. 'Do people recognize you in this area?' I ask. Ali shoots me a fierce look, and grins: 'Everyone in the world recognizes me,' he says. Just then, we pull up at the traffic light. A group of schoolboys, crossing in front of the bus, looks up at us through the windshield. Suddenly their mouths fall open, and they start waving.

Some twenty minutes later, as the bus heads back towards camp, we fall into conversation about Ali's travels through the world. 'I

been all over the place,' he says. 'I met Nasser. He embraced me on the steps of the capital; it brought tears to my eyes. I thought, "Here I am, this little boy from Louisville, standing with one of the great leaders of the world."

'But I'd never live anywhere but the United States. Just look at this country! There's more hotels, better restaurants . . . You don't see a six-lane highway in the middle of nowhere anywhere else in the world.' He grins to himself. 'And there's more ice here! You can get it whenever you want it! If you want a coke, you got a cold coke! As cooooooooold as you want! You can get ice any time!'

'Why do you think I cry?' "Because you care about him so much,' I answered. Bundini's face relaxed into a broad energetic smile and he shook hands with me, saying, 'You're right. You understand. You got it. That's nice. Real Kosher.'

Then again his mood changes suddenly. 'But America's dying. You see a tragedy every day,' he says, turning the bus off the road and uphill slowly into camp.

Next time I saw Bundini, I mentioned the incident to him. 'Don't it mess you up?' he said.

'You burst into tears at the end of the fight in L.A.' I said. 'I saw a picture of you in the newspaper.'

'Yeah,' Bundini breathed, grinning. 'Why do you think I cry?'

'Because you care about him so much,' I answered.

Bundini's face relaxed into a broad energetic smile and he shook hands with me, saying, 'You're right. You understand. You got it. That's nice. Real Kosher.'

One evening during the last hot summer of Watergate, I called Ali to ask if he thought President Nixon should be impeached. I had never asked him such an overtly political question and, uncertain of his response, we chatted briefly about the camp before letting

81

the impeachment question fall.

Sure enough, Ali was not interested. 'My wisdom is too limited to judge a man in such a great position,' he said. 'So I don't want to say nothing about that, and it is not my business and not my country.'

'You don't think it's important?'

'I feel there ain't no more important thing than the black people the government's been mistreating every day. There ain't no more important thing than the black people who was robbed, whom the government brought over here. There ain't no more important than us. Than the Muslims in my religion shot and killed daily by police throughout the country. So it's just a case of white people judging white people, because white people were crooked to white people.'

'But don't you think the Watergate situation . . .' I broke in.

'I don't know nothing about Watergate,' Ali countered. 'I just know what I hear on T.V., and I don't follow that closely. To me, the country's always been in lies and thieves, so it ain't no surprise to me this happened. My phone is tapped now. Elijah Muhammad's phone is tapped . . .

His voice trailed off. 'So how are you feeling, Ali?' I asked.

'I'm feeling good.'

BLUEBIRDS FLY
WITH BLUEBIRDS

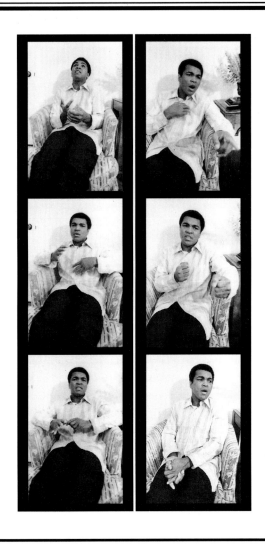

BLUEBIRDS FLY WITH BLUEBIRDS

arrived in camp the next afternoon at about 3:00. As I rounded the first cabin, walking slowly toward the courtyard, I could see smoke curling up from the far side of the camp. To the left of Ali's cabin, past his green Rolls parked in the center of the courtyard, Angelo and Blood were burning garbage in a large wire container. I sat on top of a rock and watched the thick smoke roll down off the hill.

Soon Ali appeared and beckoned us over to join him in the shadow of Coretta's kitchen.

'So you've been watching the Watergate hearings on T.V.?' we asked, taking a seat beside him on a long wooden bench.

'No, not really,' Ali replied, bending down to pick up some pebbles. 'They just crooks. I knew that already.'

'So what have you been doing since I last saw you?'

'Well, I got some new writings,' he said. 'Some beautiful short poems.' He stood up and, running over to the Rolls, pulled open the rear door. Emerging from the back seat with a sheaf of paper, he danced back grinning to the bench and sat down beside me with the pages in both hands, ready to read. There were some twenty-five pieces of Fighter's Heaven stationary, with a small picture of Ali at the bottom of each page.

'These are some one-line things that I think I'm going to put on signs. People can hang them up in the kitchen, they can put

them on their walls.' As Ali gestured, making an imaginary kitchen wall with his left hand, I glanced over his right shoulder at the writing. The pages were covered with poems scrawled on both sides in large, spiderish handwriting. 'I prefer you don't read, just listen,' he suggested politely but firmly, arranging the pile of papers neatly in his lap.

I nodded and sat back as he began to read, looking up confidently to repeat each 'poem' a second time slowly, emphatically, before he'd glance down for another line. The first one went:

A worldly loss often turns into spiritual gain. 'Many people lost Martin Luther King but – I hate to say it – it helped people to get more things they wanted,' Ali commented. 'I gave up my title and money for four years, and now I'm bigger than ever and more praised and well-respected and honored. See? Beautiful!' We nodded as he fished down into his lap for another one-line poem, came up with it, and read:

86 **The man who is not courageous enough to take risks will**

'Many people lost Martin Luther King but – I hate to say it – it helped people to get more things they wanted,' Ali commented. 'I gave up my title and money for four years, and now I'm bigger than ever and more praised and well-respected and honored. See? Beautiful!'

accomplish nothing in life. 'I take a lot of risks with odds against me,' Ali explained; 'predictions, the draft, my religion, my name. I mean, the man who went to the moon didn't have to come back. Columbus went around the world, and they thought he would fall off. See? The man who is not courageous enough to take risks will accomplish nothing in life. Beautiful!'

'Now here's a good one,' he continued. 'Here's one of my favorites:

False politeness is like imitation jewelry, and false kisses are like imitation flowers. 'Ain't that beautiful?' he sighed.

The spirit of controversy is fed through argument. 'And that's why me and Howard Cosell are a controversy, 'cause we're always arguing!'

Every moment of your life is more valuable than anything else in the world. 'All the diamonds in the world, this car, this camp, my title – every moment is more valuable. If you don't believe it, let me hold my hand over your mouth for three minutes, and you'd die. See? These moments are valuable. Beautiful!'

One cannot be wise and foolish at the same time, for light and darkness cannot do well together.

'Does that apply to integration, too?' I asked.

Ali paused. 'Sure. There are more white women after negroes now than ever. Go to a discotheque in New York and watch what's happening: everybody sitting with their integrated mate. That ain't nothing. That's bad. Bastard children. No intelligent white man or white woman in his or her right mind wants black boys and black girls marrying their sons and daughters, introducing their grandchildren as half-brown, kinky haired negroes. They don't want that. No black man, no black woman, in his or her right mind, wants any white boys or white girls marrying their beautiful black sons and daughters, introducing their grandchildren as blond haired half-negroes. It's embarrassing. Every man wants a child to look like himself.

'The Japanese love their little Japanese children; Eskimos love their little Eskimo children. I love my daughters and my son, and they look like me. I don't want no blond haired, blue eyed son. That ain't progress. Spotted up, losing identity . . .

'The Chinese love China, the Mexicans love Mexico, the Hindus love India. They love the culture. Who wants to lose themselves through blood-mating? You come back twenty years later, you don't know who is who. That ain't progress; that's fighting God.

'Bluebirds fly with bluebirds, pigeons like pigeons, eagles like eagles, buzzards like buzzards. All of them are birds, but they have different hangouts. Flies are with flies, you see bees with bees: insects got sense. Now why are negroes and white people in America so right, and all of nature wrong? Blue birds fly with blue birds and red birds with red birds, and if the blue bird get lost with the red bird, he get on out. You see the black ant dragging the other ants to get out of his neighborhood; they even fight.

'Everything wants to be with his own kind, except the negroes, who don't know themselves, and the white people, who are trying to trick the negroes into thinking that 400-year-old enemies are all of a sudden brothers. Old white man in Mississippi, now all of a sudden you can go and get his daughter, take her out and screw her. You know that old man, that didn't like niggers five years ago, ain't changed now. No! You can do anything you want now, down South. I could take a white girl right now, walk her downtown Mississippi, hold her in my hands, and won't nobody say nothing. That change is too quick.

'But the government sends out pamphlets. They know they gotta . . . The only way Pharoah could stay alive was to keep the slaves in Egypt. As soon as black people got out of Egypt, then Pharoah was in trouble. As long as black people are in America, she won't have too many problems; but as soon as they separate, or even start thinking of splitting, there's going to be a lot of trouble. So the government don't want this, so they are stopping it through integration. They got fresh air programs down there

89

"See, what's going to happen is, like a woman's nine months' pregnant, and the baby starts kicking, and the baby wants to get out. Well, if they don't get that baby out, the woman and the baby will die. Well America, she is pregnant with the truth."

where they send little black boys from the North to the South and into the white town. And you know that's phony; it's hypocritical. What's a white family in Alabama doing with a little black boy? Here's the little black boy, eight years old, and the little white girl is twelve, and they're running around playing. What's that going to lead up to? That ain't no good. And the white family's taking care of the black boy; you know that's not real. It's something that's being pushed by the government.

"I respect you. I treat everybody good, integrate. We're integrating now. But I ain't going to go drinking with your woman!"

'See, I got a plan here. When I retire, I'm gonna have black boys from the ghetto come out here. Now that's good, a summer camp where black children can be with their own kind; none of this forced integration like they have now.

'See, America's going to be so plagued with draughts and tornadoes and earthquakes and hurricanes and beef and food, milk and all kinds of shortages, that God is going to force America to let black people go free, separate. See, what's going to happen is, like a woman's nine months' pregnant, and the baby starts kicking, and the baby wants to get out. Well, if they don't get that baby out, the woman and the baby will die. Well America, she is pregnant with the truth. In 1930, the seed of truth was planted. Allah God, a flesh and blood man, came to America, taught Elijah Muhammad, told him to unite black people, bring them back to Islam, back to their right names, cultures, religion. America's rule is over; it's time for us to separate. Now this truth has been planted and it's growing. The baby, the black man, is now kicking; he wants to be free. America's paining. And if she don't let him go, they'll both die.

'But you know, it's not hate. I don't hate nobody. I know people. I know where to go, where not to go. I know whose daughter to look at, whose daughter not to look at. I don't get in no trouble. The man in trouble is the man who don't know where he is. The man in Vietnam who knows how to find a booby trap is in less trouble than the man who can't find a booby trap.

'I respect you. I treat everybody good, integrate. We're integrating now. But I ain't going to go drinking with your woman! That's going too far. Too many pretty black women that I could meet, Chinese or Mexicans or Puerto Ricans or Saudi Arabians or Turks or Algerians or Indonesians. They all dark, all

91

Asiatic. I can marry a Mexican woman, ain't nobody going to be mad. I can marry an African woman, ain't nobody gonna be mad. I can marry an Egyptian woman; I been offered all kinds of women in the Moslem world. I can marry a Pakistani woman; they're beautiful people – complexion, hair . . . Why do I want to go out of my way chasing after someone when her brother might shoot me or poison me? It's sick. See, this ain't no progress. It's gonna be stopped. Black people are gonna be Muslims soon. They all gonna be with Elijah Muhammad. But the white man, who is the most powerful, will have to kinda get weak. And when they see that he ain't so big and bad, then they'll come and follow. The power will be broke. See, the black people are like leeches on a dog's back, sucking his blood. The dog die, the leech die. So the leech has to find another back to hop on to. See?

'So if you notice the country, you notice the way the money's falling. You turn on the news at six o'clock: all bad news. Look at the meat problem, the concrete problem, the war and . . . See, America's like a rich person who's poor, but they have a lot of food in the frigidaire. But all they got is what's in the frige, and as soon as the frigidaire be empty, that's real trouble. But she still pretending to be big and powerful, red white and blue. But she's got just a little left in the frigidaire, and when that's gone, that's it.

'See, America, they haven't been here but a few years. Look at the history. America's been here for two hundred years. What's two hundred years? The Gaza pyramid in Egypt is 7500 years old. I mean, America just got here yesterday. People are intoxicated with narcotics, alcohol, and some with wealth. America's so intoxicated, she really believes that she's God. A little airplane gets up there in a thunderstorm, and you can't fly. In Chicago the other day, there was a rainstorm. The airport wasn't worth a quarter, the radar wasn't worth a quarter, the big bad jets . . . Just a little rain. Now say there is somebody out there who could control that, on earth. Look how powerful that is. A little snow could come – you can't get in this camp, you can't get up this hill. A little snow.'

NO WHITE MAN'S GONNA TREAT ME LIKE A
NIGGER NO MORE

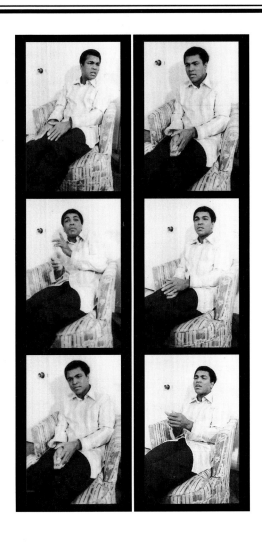

NO WHITE MAN'S GOING TO TREAT ME LIKE A NIGGER NO MORE

A **dark blue Cadillac limousine** turns down the drive, gliding to a stop beside the gym, and a fair-haired balding man in light gray trousers and a blue blazer climbs out, followed by a group of long-haired white men carrying camera equipment in black leather cases. Taking the keys from the chauffeur, one of the young men opens the trunk and quickly begins to unload more cameras and lighting equipment, calling out to the others, who stand by nervously, helpless: 'Percy, pass me that lens ... Terry, get the stuff from the back seat . . . Robin, here, grab this will you? . . . Larry, hold this now . . .'

I step up cautiously and stand just behind the young man identified as Percy: 'Excuse me, what is going on?'

'We're B.B.C.,' Percy explains. 'Excuse me . . .' and he pushes past me through the door. I follow him in.

'So what are you gonna do?' I ask, stopping beside him as he stoops to open a large black case.

'We are filming a documentary on Arthur Ashe for the B.B.C.,

the British Broadcasting Corporation . . .' he begins, struggling with the lock. 'Mr. Ashe will be here soon, and then we shall interview him and Mr. Ali together.'

Around me the crew has begun to set up their lights. The balding man has removed his blue blazer and is now rushing about in a transparent cotton shirt, giving orders to the young men, pointing this way and that with a small wooden baton: 'Swing that over here, Terry . . . Perfect! Perfect! Just like that . . . very good. Robin, can you manage that light? . . . That's fine . . . Oh yes . . . Super! Just there . . .'

Behind us, the door swings open and Angelo darts in with his right hand outstretched, looking for the man in charge. The director turns: 'Ah!' he exclaims. 'You are Mr. . . . ?'

'Dundee,' Angelo says, stepping over to the director's outstretched hand. 'Ali's manager.'

'Why certainly, yes . . .' The men drift off along the wall, avoiding the cameras, talking politely in subdued voices. I back off slowly and sit down outside the door.

95

Fifteen minutes pass, and a second blue Cadillac arrives and glides to a stop behind the first. The rear door opens slowly and Arthur Ashe emerges dressed in Ivy collegiate style – thin, handsome, with long graceful hands and a manicured smile. He glances down at me briefly then steps past me into the spotlit gym. I get up and follow him in.

'Arthur!' the B.B.C. director shouts, hurrying along the wall to greet Ashe. 'Where have you been?'

'We got lost,' Ashe explains.

'Oh dear! No! Where?'

Ashe shrugs. 'I don't know. We kept asking people, and they all said, "Just down the road."'

The director smiles: 'Well, here you are.' He takes Ashe by the arm, guiding him back along the wall towards Angelo, who is again standing with his right hand outstretched. 'Arthur, this is Mr. Dunday. Mr. Dunday, Arthur Ashe.'

'Dundee,' Angelo says, nodding three times.

'Hello,' says Ashe. The three move across the ring and stand

'I'm always available! I'm always available!' Ali shouts. 'Just call me up and I'll find time for you! I'm nice to people! He who makes room in his heart will find accommodation everywhere, that's what I say. That's me. You come up here, I got time for you!'

facing out toward the camera, talking quietly. Ashe is totally cool.

Suddenly the side door swings open quickly, and Ali strides in, beaming. Bundini fans out to his left, Blood to his right, and they move quickly to the center of the room. The B.B.C. crew looks up, startled.

Angelo leads Ashe and the director over to where Ali stands. Everyone crowds around as they shake hands. 'I didn't think we'd be able to see you,' Ashe begins, striking a cocktail party pose. 'We were filming down in the Bahamas when somebody suggested it would be good to do something with you and me together, but I

97

didn't even think we should bother to try. Thought you'd be much too busy training . . .'

'I'm always available! I'm always available!' Ali shouts. 'Just call me up and I'll find time for you! I'm nice to people! He who makes room in his heart will find accommodation everywhere, that's what I say. That's me. You come up here, I got time for you!'

Ashe has recently been in the headlines for refusing to play before a segregated audience in South Africa. This tenuous political thread is about all that spans the vast gap between Ashe and Ali, but the B.B.C. director has decided it will hold up well under the spotlights, and he quickly moves the two men into place, posing them side by side on a wooden table next to the ring. He draws up a chair to one side of the table and sits down quickly to begin. After a final check, the cameras roll.

Doubling as an interviewer, the director reads an introduction from file cards concealed in his lap, telling the audience that these two men are similar in that they are both black, athletes, and controversial. Then he drops his notes and turns to Ashe: 'Arthur Ashe, you were recently invited to play in South Africa. Would you tell us a little about your visit?'

'Yes,' Ashe says, leaning toward the camera, speaking clearly, sounding young. He is sitting on his hands. 'They invited me, but I said I wouldn't play in front of a segregated audience. They wrote and said they'd arrange for me to visit black leaders in Johannesburg, and they'd let me go around with them and inspect the conditions freely. So, as an official visitor from the United States, but in the care of some black leaders, I did finally make the

Muhammad Ali, if you were asked to fight in South Africa, would you go?'...No whitey! No white man's gonna treat me like a nigger no more!' He wraps his right hand around the director's throat. The director blanches and pulls back nervously.

visit. I'm sorry my stay was so short, but it was interesting to go around, and I met some very nice people with whom I'm still in touch. . .'

Ashe goes on like this for a few minutes while Ali stares stonily at the ground, his hands folded loosely in his lap. Finally the director, hoping to involve Ali in this quiet discussion of the South African situation, turns to him and says jovially: 'Muhammad Ali, if you were asked to fight in South Africa, would you go?'

Ali snaps into action as if an electric shock has run through his body. His feet hit the ground and in one stride he crosses the space between the table and the director's chair with his left hand raised above his head, his right hand swooping in toward the man's jugular, screaming: 'No whitey! No white man's gonna treat me like a nigger no more!' He wraps his right hand around the director's throat. The director blanches and pulls back nervously. Ali holds him for a second then steps back, grins down at him, and, as the cameras zero in for closeups on his face, launches into a shortened version of the Bluebirds speech he made to me before. For a moment, the director stares up at Ali in horror, but gradually he understands, gasping, 'Do that some more!' He sits up and straightens his tie.

When he has finished his monologue, Ali sits back beside Ashe, who nods at him with a vague, embarrassed smile. As if it were the end of a cricket match, the B.B.C. crew applauds lightly; their director edges back up in his chair to ask Ashe a few more polite questions.

The interview never quite gets off the ground again. Ali returns to his former stony silence, and Ashe, in an attempt to re-establish his shattered link with Ali, becomes non-commital, even terse, as if he feels his own black power again. After a few short observations on the magnitude of the event, the director raises his baton and the session draws to a close.

As the cameras stop, Ali stands up, smiling and friendly. 'Bundini!' he calls out.

Bundini comes over. 'Let me get some pictures of you now, okay?' he says. His arm on Ashe's shoulder, Ali poses, smiling, while Bundini snaps away. Then, with a big wave, followed by his entourage, Ali turns and walks slowly out of the gym.

THIS 20TH CENTURY
EXUBERANCE

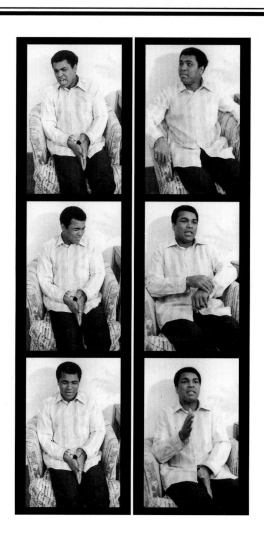

THIS 20TH CENTURY EXUBERANCE

li is a boxer and a talker, an athlete and an intellectual, a teacher and leader and religious man, a poet and joker; builder, philosopher, father, husband, friend, politician and millionaire. He is the clearcut product of common sense and hard work. He is also a mystery man who combines a vast amount of media savvy with bragadaccio and innate timing. The only umbrella for all these qualities is the teachings of Elijah Muhammad.

'Ali is like a man who can write beautifully, but doesn't know how to punctuate,' says Archie Moore. 'Sometimes he sounds humorous, sometimes he sounds like Ezra Pound's poetry. He has this 20th century exuberance, but there is a bitterness somewhere.'

Ali might sooner agree with Mao Tse-tung: 'Our purpose is to ensure that literature operates as a powerful weapon for uniting and educating the people and helps the people to fight the enemy with one heart and one mind.' As he leaves the ring, Ali emerges as a champion of a cause – 'The People's Champion' as he has always claimed to be, using his fame and charisma to move off after new horizons.

'My fights are leaving the sports world and going to countries,'

he announced at the official opening of Fighter's Heaven.

To accomplish this, Ali must undergo a fundamental change. Having attained a symbolic position of leadership to millions of people around the world, he must now sublimate himself to the message he is assigned to transmit on behalf of Elijah Muhammad and the Black Muslim faith, becoming the servant of that message which passes through him to be amplified, teaching practically (by the example of his life) and theoretically (by his essays and poems) how black people around the world can help themselves to be financially independent and emotionally strong. He leaves the ring under a great burden of responsibility.

Sometimes small incidents at the camp revealed a tension which is all but hidden to the casual observer, as on my last day.

I'm sitting with Gene Kilroy, looking out over the hills, when Ali appears. He waves and walks across to join us by the rocks, one of which has a natural seat carved into it by years of erosion. He stops in front of the rock: 'This rock is dirty!' he says, leaning forward and scraping leaves and earth out of the cracks. 'Look at all this dirt! Gotta keep my rocks clean!' He walks back to the center of the courtyard, picks up a long green garden hose and drags it across the ground, yelling for Gene to turn it on. Motioning, Gene aside, Ali begins to hose down the rock. For

...the gym door creaks open and Blood yells out: 'Ali, there's a call from Africa! Man wants to talk to you!' Ali frowns slightly, walks back to turn off the hose, then looks up slowly and shouts back: 'Tell him I'm not here! Tell him to call back Tuesday!'

a long time, he keeps spraying – absorbed, distracted, moving to another rock as soon as the first is clean – while I stand with Gene, watching. After twenty minutes of silence, Gene walks back across the courtyard to his station wagon, which is parked near the kitchen.

Suddenly Ali looks over his shoulder and yells: 'Hey Gene! Bring the gun!'

'Okay Muhammad,' Gene yells, and he disappears around the side of the gym, returning three minutes later with a large new revolver.

'Load it for me,' Ali says, still training the hose on a rock. Gene

quickly loads the revolver and hands it to Ali. Ali hands the hose to Gene, steps to the ledge of the hill and, stretching his arm out straight, points the gun down into the trees. He fires abruptly three times without flinching. I stare at him nervously, uncertain what to make of this.

As the smoke drifts off, Ali turns and, catching me staring at him, wheels back toward Gene: 'Put it up!' he snaps. Gene steps forward, shielding the gun from my sight, takes it from Ali's hand and, dropping the hose, walks quickly away. Without looking at me Ali picks up the hose and continues washing the rocks.

After a few minutes, the gym door creaks open and Blood yells out: 'Ali, there's a call from Africa! Man wants to talk to you!' Ali frowns slightly, walks back to turn off the hose, then looks up slowly and shouts back: 'Tell him I'm not here! Tell him to call back Tuesday!' Blood waves and turns back inside. Ali is holding the hose in the palm of his hand; a little water drips out. 'No, tell him Thursday!' he shouts suddenly. Blood reappears and looks around. 'Okay!' he yells, and disappears again through the door. Ali goes back to the rocks.

'FRAID
OF NOTHING

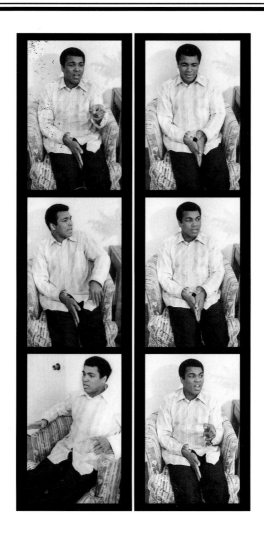

'FRAID OF NOTHING

Later, knowing that I will not be seeing him again for a while, I take the opportunity to ask Ali a couple of questions that have been on my mind since the Arthur Ashe meeting.

'Are you ever afraid of anything?'

'No sir. 'fraid of nothing,' he says quickly. 'We have a saying in the faith: "True Muslims neither fear, nor do they grieve." That's a true religious thought, we neither fear nor do we grieve. I don't fear nothing, nor do I grieve about nothing.'

'What are you gonna do after you retire?'

'Well, most likely I'll go back to ministering the Muslim faith, spreading it through America.'

'You'll do that as a full time occupation?'

'That's my main goal.'

'How will you go about it? Lecturing? Travelling around?'

'That's up to our leader, the honorable Elijah Muhammad. He's gonna give me an assignment, where to go, what to do, either to serve at the mosque or temple in one city, or else to do a lot of travelling around, studying. I got to get a lot more lessons from him.'

Trying to imagine Ali settled in one place for a long time, I say: 'If you're running a mosque, what kind of things would you do on a daily basis?'

**'Do you ever wish that you weren't famous?'
'Right,' Ali answers without a moment's hesitation.**

'Meetings three times a week, and Sundays. That's all. But I'd prefer travelling, if I can get the honor to do that – more of a Billy Graham type thing: travel throughout the world and country, spread the word of Islam.'

'So what do you think is the biggest strength you have as a person, what gives you this Art of Personality, makes you able to do something like Billy Graham?'

'The teachings of Elijah Muhammad. I've been involved in this now for fourteen years and this is developing more and more each day.'

'But obviously everyone who's taught by him doesn't have the same ability to go out and spread the word.'

'Right. Well, naturally, boxing is what causes that, my influence in the sport world and recognition up there. That's what makes me more popular than anybody else.'

'But all these magazines point out that even without the boxing ring, it's your personality that draws the crowd.'

'Yeah, the poems, the gimmicks, the predictions, the arrogance, the way I act.'

'Do you ever wish that you weren't famous?'

'Right,' Ali answers without a moment's hesitation.

'You wish that when you retire from boxing, you would be a less famous person?'

'Famous for one reason: to help others, to draw crowds, to promote, propagate the faith. But otherwise I wish nobody knew me.'

After supper, Ali walked slowly to the kitchen door: 'Ah, it's good stuff,' he sighed. 'Everything I'm studying now. It's beautiful. I never heard it in my life before, and I don't think there's nowhere else you can see it. It's gonna inspire people.' He stretched out his hand. I said goodbye and turned to go. As I rounded the edge of the gym, he called out again, 'Goodnight fella!' Turning, I saw him framed for a moment in the light of the kitchen door. Then he stepped back and was gone.

LAST VISIT TO FIGHTER' HEAVEN: THREE ROUNDS WITH
ANDY WARHOL

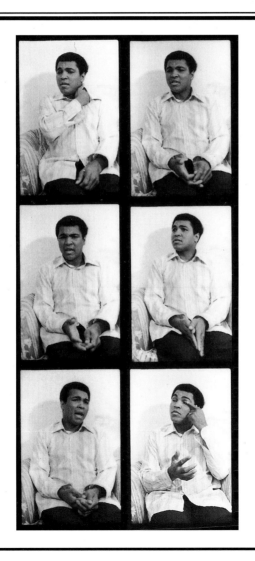

THREE ROUNDS WITH
ANDY WARHOL

n his fiftieth year, 1977, Warhol completed, in three months, a series of ten portraits of America's greatest athletes; O.J. Simpson, Rod Gilbert, Dorothy Hamill, Jack Nicklaus, Willie Shoemaker, Tom Seaver, Chris Evert, Pelé, Kareem Abdul-Jabbar . . . One of the people he was bound to paint was Muhammad Ali. Since I am particularly interested in the parallels between Ali and Warhol (once writing in Al Goldstein's *National Screw,* 'Who does Andy Warhol remind you of most? Muhammad Ali.'), I felt sure that the meeting would be well worth recording.

On the morning of Tuesday, August 16th, at 10 a.m., we arrived at Ali's spacious log cabin camp to find it almost deserted. A solitary Ernest Borgnine–style black aid

Photographs by Victor Bockris

explained that Ali had arrived from London on the Concorde the previous night and checked into his log cabin. A small new light green Mercedes was parked next to it. He was expecting us at ten and scheduled to start training for the fight against Ernie Shavers at 2 p.m.

Waiting for Ali to emerge, Andy and Fred looked for an area to take the polaroids. They needed a white backdrop. Gene Kilroy – one of Ali's friendliest aids – hung a damp white sheet over the

As we walked, he told me that he'd just been in Gottenberg, Sweden, talking to 23,000 people on a talkathon. 'They paid me $20,000 for four hours.'

bathroom door in the gymnasium, and Fred put a metal chair in front of it. Then Andy remembered he'd left all the cameras and film in his limousine, which we could see slowly pulling out of the parking lot and heading down the hill to refuel. 'Gee, we almost came for nothing,' he said, and ran out to stop the driver.

After everything was set up, we waited five minutes in the dirt clearing between the gym and Ali's log cabin, chatting with a couple of aids, until he came out, wearing black boots, black pants and a black shirt. He looked a little heavy.

Ali shook Andy's hand without looking at him, then said, 'Come on, let's go across to the gym.' As we walked, he told me that he'd just been in Gottenberg, Sweden, talking to 23,000 people on a talkathon. 'They paid me $20,000 for four hours.'

Ali led us through his dressing room – Andy stopped to admire the boxing trunks, robe, jockstrap and other equipment laid out on the rubbing table – into the gym, where he silently slumped on to the brown metal chair in front of the white sheet and stared moodily at the floor. He had, Gene Kilroy warned us, pretty bad jet lag from thirteen days flying around Europe. To his left, a nine-foot-tall portrait by Leroy Neiman was painted on the wall. To his right, Andy had laid out the three cameras and a polythene package of films on a green plastic couch.

...some animation came into Ali's face as he started remembering howhow the London blacks begged him to lead them in the riots: 'Fifteen minutes after I told them "No" in my suite at the Hilton,' he laughed, 'they were over in Notting Hill fighting the police. I can't be responsible for starting no trouble in somebody else's country . . .'

Warhol slowly began to take pictures, but Ali was unusually uncooperative. He either looked at the floor, or away from the camera. He would not rise to the occasion. I asked Kilroy if Ali knew who Warhol was. Yes. But his recent publicity tour of Europe had alerted him to the fact that the influence of his name across the world had reached proportions that surprised even him, and so, as Andy angled for a good position, I began asking questions.

In a few minutes, some animation crept into Ali's face as he started remembering how the mounted police had to rescue him from crowds in Sweden by putting him on a horse, how the people of South Africa had sent a representative to thirteen cities across Europe looking for him to beg him to be their leader, how all the archbishops in England wanted him to preach in their churches, how 20,000 people mobbed him at the Houses of

115

"Champ . . . do you think you could . . . remove your . . . shirt?"

Parliament and how the London blacks begged him to lead them in the riots: 'Fifteen minutes after I told them "No" in my suite at the Hilton,' he laughed, 'they were over in Notting Hill fighting the police. I can't be responsible for starting no trouble in somebody else's country . . .'

After a fifteen-minute monologue, during which Ali continued to pay no attention to Warhol, who was repeatedly snapping polaroids of his talking profile, Fred Hughes gingerly asked: 'Champ . . . do you think you could . . . remove your . . . shirt?'

(Fred said afterwards that he was terrified Ali might refuse.)

Immediately looking bored again (with a 'who do these suckers think I am' expression) Ali grudgingly complied, shrugging off the black silk shirt to reveal several tires of fat around his stomach. He said it was good to have fifteen pounds to lose because it made him work harder and he would be down to 220 for the fight. Then, as Andy continued to take the pictures, Ali asked, 'How much these paintings gonna sell for?'

'$25,000,' answered Hughes. 'Can you turn yourself a little bit towards the camera, champ?'

'Who could they get to pay $25,000 for a picture?' asked Ali incredulously.

'He's sold quite a few pictures for more than that.'

'Well, I guess if you do it real fancy,' he admitted. 'I started out making $4.00 for my first fight. But imagine paying $25,000 for a painting!'

'We should have brought down one of Andy's black drag queens,' whispered Fred. 'They went for $28,000 each.'

But Ali was still trying to work out the equation. He started talking about God and came to the conclusion that, 'Man is more attractive than anything else. Look at me! White people gonna pay $25,000 for my picture! This little negro from Kentucky couldn't buy a $1,500 motorcycle a few years ago and now they pay $25,000 for my picture!'

After another fifteen-minute Alilogue on 'subtle discrimination

He started talking about God and came to the conclusion that, 'Man is more attractive than anything else. Look at me! White people gonna pay $25,000 for my picture! This little negro from Kentucky couldn't buy a $1500 motorcycle a few years ago and now they pay $25,000 for my picture!'

117

against blacks in Swedish nightclubs,' (involving an incident in which Ali took 23 black Africans into a Swedish nightclub and ordered steaks for all of them to be served on the dancefloor), Andy interrupted: 'Could we do some where you're not . . . er, talking, just . . . just?'

It may have been the first time in years anyone outside the ring has told the champ to shut up. There was total silence. Warhol recalled: 'I guess I really had told the Champ to shut up. He just stared at the floor. I thought he was going to punch me.' Ali paused, then, smiling ruefully said, 'Yeah, well yeah.' (Hanging his head.) 'I'm sorry. I should be (laughing quietly to himself) doing your job. You paying me.' And he flipped through a series of boxing poses;

Andy Just like that, that's really great. Just a couple more.

Ali I wish you could take pictures in five weeks when I get more trim, a little more prettier.

Andy Just three more.

Ali How about this? (Raises both fists.)

Andy That's great. Could you put both fists close to your face, closer to your face . . . more.

Ali Do I look fearless?

Andy Very fearless. That's fantastic!

A nervous aid, concerned about the amount of energy the champ was expending on his first day of training, attempted to dismiss us when the session was over. 'Well, that wraps it up, thank you very much.'

'Thanks . . . er, champ,' said Andy, nervously extending a thin hand.

Ali spun around: 'Did you say tramp?'

'No . . . I . . .'

'I have more fun with that,' he laughed. 'I'm on the streets and a fellow see me and say "CHAMP!" I say, "Did you say tramp?" And he say (screaming) "NO, NO, NO, I SAID CHAMP!" Come on!' Ali was beginning to enjoy himself. 'I'm gonna show you my

I tried to initiate a conversation – 'Well, you know, Ali, Andy makes movies as well. You're really interested in going into movies, aren't you?'

mosque. Want you to meet my wife . . .'

We took some more pictures out by the mosque. Ali was very concerned about getting the right features of the mosque in the background, and, at one point, after looking through the viewfinder of my pentax to see what I was getting, admonished, 'I don't think you getting the right pictures.'

Then we went across to his wife's cabin, but she wouldn't come out from behind the screen door because she wasn't dressed

119

properly and didn't have on any make-up. So she asked Ali to take care of the kid for a while. He likes holding babies.

Then Ali remembered that he had a poem he wanted to read Andy. As we walked back past the gym along the path leading to his log cabin, I tried to initiate a conversation – 'Well, you know, Ali, Andy makes movies as well. You're really interested in going into movies, aren't you?' – but, looking horrified, Warhol ducked into the gym – 'to check on the polaroids I'll be right back' – and Ali just looked even more bored.

The rest of the way over to his cabin he mumbled about Hollywood. 'I predict they'll never want a good black movie. *Blackula*! *Cotton Goes to Harlem*! *Nigger Charlie*! (mumble mumble mumble)!'

Inside the single-room log cabin, Andy rejoined us and Ali proudly pointed out his enormous double bed, which he got in L.A. for $1100, then flopped into an armchair behind a low table covered with stacks of index cards, notebooks, sheets of paper and pens. Three open briefcases stood on the floor to his left. Andy perched on the edge of a small wooden chair opposite him. Everyone gathered around as Ali fished a large hand into one of the briefcases, came up with a single sheet of lined notepaper covered with blue biro scrawl and read:

Concorde's Palace

I was flying the Concorde at 60,000 feet
And the feeling you get is really neat.
It puts everything New York has to a pity
So to keep it looking bad they keep it out of the city.
The Americans should be protesting to save the young boys
Instead of wasting time protesting the Concorde's noise.
The Concorde is the greatest thing in the history of mankind.
When headed in the right direction it outruns the sunshine.
The Americans left England years ago in order to be free
So they should remember that the people made the Concorde
Out of the roots of their tree.

Fred Hughes and Courtney Sale on the Rock at Fighter's Heaven.

Then, without pausing, he leaned forward, started playing with a particularly thick stack of index cards, looked across at Andy, and began speaking at him rapidly:

'I ask you why we're having so much crime in the world . . .

'Rape is high across the country. Prostitution. Homosexuality – they marchin'. You shocked to see so many of them, the gay people of all kind you got I mean . . . everything just goin' wild. There's no moral upliftment.

"You go to N.Y.C. and see everything in the movies, every act, oral sex, you sit there and watch it. And the magazine stands are so filthy you cain't even walk by with your children."

Bockras and Ali pick up where they left off 3 years earlier.

'Women with their legs wide open, two men screwing each other right on a magazine stand! You can walk down the street and duck in a movie and watch them screwing. Little child sixteen years old go in can watch them screwing and he's too young to get his own sex so he gotta rape somebody, he gotta watch the movie. You go to N.Y.C. and see everything in the movies, every act, oral sex, you sit there and watch it. And the magazine stands are so filthy you cain't even walk by with your children.'

(SCREAMING) 'Right? Walk down the street and look at it you got children! Women are screwing women! No faith. Man has lost faith in man.

'Look, you taking my picture for $25,000. You gonna give me $15,000 for the few minutes. $15,000 you give me to come and take two or three pictures. $15,000! The average working man, it'd be good if he got that a year. You gonna give this little black boy $15,000 for sitting there for three minutes! Well, hell, how much more valuable is me making a prayer somewhere for no money? And prostitution. You got gangs, you got war, you got crimes, you got murder. I got the name, the world's waiting for me!

"You're a person of wisdom and you can travel and spread the news. I'm telling you that the world hasn't seen nothing yet! They just seen a little exercise, but now they gonna see ME!"

'I'm not getting on you, but I'm gonna make you feel like a kindergarten child. This black boxer here will make you feel like a kindergarten child. I gave this here' – and he hauled out the stack of index cards – 'lecture to the English Parliament (I think this has to be a mistake, but it is what he said) the day before yesterday, it's called The Real Cause of Man's Distress and it'll only take 12½ minutes.'

(Speaking directly to Warhol). 'You're a person of wisdom and you can travel and spread the news. I'm telling you that the world hasn't seen nothing yet! They just seen a little exercise, but now they gonna see ME!' Ali sat back in his chair, peeled off the rubber band, and began to read through the cards.

For an uninterrupted forty-five minutes he careened through a wide variety of Muslim sayings, 'down home' sayings, imitations, digressions, and constant repetitions. At his best, Muhammad is a master of oratory. He has a beautiful voice, hands and face – the essential tools of a public speaker – and he can work all three

123

Throughout the sermon, Andy stared blankly into space, – 'I wanted to change the subject but I didn't know how' – Fred Hughes hung desperately on to a bedpost, Courtney Sale kept a fixed grin going, and I tottered back and forth on my heels,

simultaneously. At his worst, he sounds like what Allen Ginsberg refers to as 'a teaheads revery'.

Ali talked about prostitution on the steps of The White House, gravity, meteorites, jumping out of windows, Israel, Egypt, Zaire, South Africa, drugs, broken skulls, delusions, angel food cake, yellow hair, Judgement Day, shattered morality, Jesus, boxing, Sweden, the Koran, friendship and . . . Elvis, relating it all to the central point that man must obey the laws of God or perish. 'I got forty-five more lectures like that,' he concluded. 'I am getting ready to go out and be a black Billy Graham.'

Throughout the sermon, Andy stared blankly into space, – 'I wanted to change the subject but I didn't know how' – Fred Hughes hung desperately on to a bedpost, Courtney Sale kept a fixed grin going, and I tottered back and forth on my heels, hunched down by Ali's feet, feeling torn between my allegiance to Andy and my allegiance to Ali, trying not to look at anyone. At one point, even Muhammad admitted that he was too tired to go on, but then some new words clicked and he whipped out another thick sheaf of papers, from a fourth briefcase hidden under his seat, and was about to wade into a major lecture on God (what he looked like, where he was, and who he was) when he was interrupted by a phone call from somebody who said he was the King of Africa.

'No, no,' said Ali. 'Tell him to call back. It ain't as important as me talking to these people here. Tell them they won't get Muhammad Ali for another hour!'

This is part of the conversation I had with Andy as we pulled out of Fighters' Heaven on the way back to Manhattan in the limousine:

Warhol What did he say? Two guys sitting on a what?

Bockris No he said two women. He just started recently talking about faggots and stuff.

Warhol Oh really? But why throw that in? That's so funny.

Bockris It just seems off the wall. He just picked up on it because he said it the last time I saw him.

Warhol Oh, because of what's her name he thinks it's the thing.

Bockris Oh, because of Anita Bryant, yeah.

Warhol Was his wife beautiful?

Bockris Oh yeah, she's very pretty. Can you imagine what it's like to be the wife of Muhammad Ali?

Warhol That baby's going to have a problem, 'cos it's going to be a big baby.

Bockris But I asked him about his other children and he says he hardly ever sees them.

Warhol But how can he preach like that? It's so crazy. I think he's a male chauvinist pig, right? He's a male chauvinist pig?

Bockris Would you prefer to have left after doing the pictures or to have sat through it?

Warhol Oh no, no, it was good to see, but it shouldn't have been so long.

Bockris On the other hand, you always said you just like to have people who talk a lot when you turn the tape recorder on.

Warhol Well listen, that's the thing. I mean, God! That's your interview. I didn't get one word, so that was the ultimate. It was the perfect interview. The nice thing is that he lets everybody come up which is kind of great.

Bockris But it does get very boring.

Warhol Well, I think he was just torturing us, but I like the way he was looking at me all the time.

Bockris He's sort of very spaced out in a way.

Warhol That's what I'm saying. He just repeats the same

125

Richard Weisman who commissioned the portrait and Ali in his dressing room at Madison Square Gardens, 1977.

simplicity over and over again and then it drums on people's ears. But he can say the things that he can because he's so good-looking that he has something more than another person does.

Bockris Well, he's been talking about being a black Billy Graham for five years now . . .

Warhol He's just holding off for the big offers. He's so young-looking still. He could be around thirty.

Bockris I don't know where he finds the energy.

Warhol He's practicing.

Bockris I felt that I should have crossed myself coming out.

Warhol We should have all repented and joined right there, it would have been . . .

Bockris It would have been so great if you could have stood up and said, 'I'll go! I'll go!'

Warhol Oh yeah. We should have done it.

Bockris I was so afraid you were going to go to sleep.

Warhol I kept thinking about things. God! Do you think he lectures his wife?

Bockris I bet he does hash over all that to her, doesn't he? He must.

Warhol Maybe he was just doing it especially for us, I don't know.

Bockris But he keeps saying he's going to do it, but he hasn't really done it yet.

Warhol He's in showbusiness. It's hard to get out. I mean, it's like, he could be threatened. But I'm surprised fighters don't take drugs, because it's just like being a rock star. You get out there and you're entertaining 30,000 people. I mean, you're a different person. I think that's why Ali feels different.

Bockris He must get bored with himself sometimes.

Warhol No, but is he intelligent? I can't figure it out.

Bockris I think he is, because he's very clever about money.

Warhol I know, but I mean – is he intelligent?

Six weeks after this visit, Ali was in New York to fight Shavers at Madison Square Garden. Richard Weissman had promised to personally deliver a copy (Andy made six) of Ali's portrait to him and Andy wanted to make the presentation two days before the fight. But Ali was so surrounded by people that it was impossible to get through to him. Finally Richard Weissman decided to take the off chance of being able to get to him at the weigh-in press conference at the Garden. He smuggled his way in with the painting, was almost thrown out by the management, but finally managed to get into the champion's dressing room and personally hand him a copy of Andy Warhol's portrait. Ali looked at it and said, 'It is by far the best painting I have ever had of myself.' Richard Weissman said, 'It's a strong painting.' Ali replied, 'I can also see a softness and compassion, as a matter of fact, I can see many moods.'